"From my father I learned to respect the past,
to respect my own heritage and myself."

*Mildred D. Taylor*

# CONTENTS

# SLAVERY...
# SEGREGATION...
# CIVIL RIGHTS...

**This section of the booklet gives a brief history of black people in America. Some more detail is given later in the booklet. *Roll of Thunder, Hear My Cry* is set in the 1930s – but it is helpful to know something of what happened *before* this period and helpful, too, to know something of what happened *after*.**

| | |
|---|---|
| 1619 | First black people brought to America |
| 1661 | Virginia legalised slavery |
| 1775 - 1783 | American War of Independence |
| | Northern states declared slavery illegal |
| 1807 | Slave trade officially abolished |
| 1831 | Slave rebellion led by Nat Turner |
| 1859 | Slave rebellion led by John Brown |
| 1861 - 1865 | American Civil War |
| 1862 | Proclamation of Emancipation |
| 1866 - 1876 | Reconstruction |
| 1866 | Ku Klux Klan formed |
| 1876 | Federal (Northern) troops withdrawn from the South |
| 1888 | Mississippi passed first segregation laws |
| 1890's - 1960's | Segregation |
| 1930's | The Depression |

# Roll of Thunder, Hear My Cry

| | |
|---|---|
| 1941 - 1945 | America in World War Two |
| 1950's & 1960's | Civil Rights Movement |
| 1954 | Supreme Court outlawed school segregation |
| 1955 | Montgomery Bus Boycott |
| 1957 | Integration of Little Rock High School |
| 1961 | Freedom Rides |
| 1963 | Civil Rights March on Washington |
| 1965 | Malcolm X murdered |
| 1968 | Assassination of Martin Luther King |
| 1972 | Angela Davis arrested |
| 1970's & 1980's | The continued fight for full equal rights |

*Born a slave, this man left the South after the Civil War. The photograph was taken in 1936.*

# Slavery

**35 to 40 million black people were taken from Africa as slaves over a period of nearly 300 years. It has been estimated that only 15 million survived the journey.**

The first slaves taken to the North American colonies from Africa were really 'indentured servants' who could gain their freedom after working a fixed period of years. But this situation did not last. By the late 17th century full slavery was widespread.

The colonies of the North, with their small farming communities already developing prosperously, did not need a large, cheap work force. The South, however was extremely fertile, but thinly settled and so needed labour. There were not enough white labourers in the South, and in any case they were not keen to do the kind of work required to develop these territories to the full. In 1661 Virginia legalised slavery and the other colonies soon followed.

Tobacco was the first major crop to draw on slave labour, quickly to be followed by rice, sugar and cotton. In ever increasing numbers, Africans were tricked, trapped, captured and cajoled into the slaving ships and in the most horrific conditions transported across the Atlantic. Chained and overcrowded below deck, many died in passage of disease, dehydration or asphyxia, their bodies being thrown into the sea. Others fought courageously with their bare hands, but their resistance was useless against heavily-armed crews. Some defiantly threw themselves into the sea rather than face a life of slavery and degradation. Charles Ball, a slave during the early 19th century, recorded the story of a slave who was brought from Africa to America:

> **At the time we came into this ship, she was full of black people, who were all confined in a dark and low place, in irons. The women were in irons as well as the men.**
>
> **About twenty persons were seized in our village at the time I was; and amongst these were the children so young that they were not able to walk or to eat any hard substance. The mothers of these children had brought them all the way with them and had them in their arms when we were taken on board this ship.**
>
> **When they put us in irons to be sent to our place of confinement in the ship, the men who fastened the irons on these mothers took the children out of their hands and threw them over the side of the ship into the water. When this was done two of the women leaped overboard after the children – the third was already confined by a chain to another woman and could not get into the water, but in struggling to disengage herself, she broke her arm and died a few days after of a fever. One of the two women who were in the river was carried down by the weight of her irons before she could be rescued; but the other was taken up by some men in a boat and brought on board. This woman threw herself overboard one night when we were at sea.**
>
> Charles Ball

---

TO BE SOLD, on board the Ship *Bance-Yland*, on tueſday the 6th of *May* next, at *Aſhley-Ferry*; a choice cargo of about 250 fine healthy

NEGROES,

juſt arrived from the Windward & Rice Coaſt. —The utmoſt care has already been taken, and ſhall be continued, to keep them free from the leaſt danger of being infected with the SMALL-POX, no boat having been on board, and all other communication with people from *Charles-Town* prevented.

*Auſtin, Laurens, & Appleby.*

*N. B.* Full one Half of the above Negroes have had the SMALL-POX in their own Country.

---

# After the Civil War: Segregation

**The American Civil War of 1861-85 was fought between the states of the North and the South. The North won — and finally ended slavery in the South. B afterwards, for many blacks, little seemed to have cha**

At the time of the American War of Independence (1775-1783), the Northern states declared slavery illegal, but the South did not. The wealth of the plantation owners in the South depended on slavery, as did the prosperity of the slave traders in Bristol and Liverpool.

In 1793 a man called Eli Whitney invented the cotton gin, a machine which successfully separated the cotton from seed and other impurities. This led to a boom in cotton production and helped also the growth of the textile industry in England. Output increased in Georgia and South Carolina, and the cotton belt spread West to Alabama, Mississippi, Louisiana and eventually to Texas.

The slave trade was officially abolished in 1807, but the Southern states continued to trade illegally. The ban had the effect of increasing the value of slaves. In some cases 'stud farms' were set up where the most able-bodied men and women were used to produce children to sell.

Slaves not only created the wealth of the South but also permanently changed the face of the countryside. They built houses, docks, bridges, roads and later railroads.

Although many Southern planters made fortunes out of cotton and slavery, in many ways their lives were made miserable by rebellious blacks. Men, women and children armed themselves and fought the plantation owners. Some quietly poisoned their masters. In their defiance, they set fire to property and sabotaged machinery and equipment. Thousands fled to the North or to Canada, and freedom.

*An artist's impression of Harriet Tubman leading a group of slaves from the South to the North using the 'Underground Railroad': a secret escape route.*

The Civil War destroyed much of the agricultural land and property in the South, and drained the region of money. There was not enough left to get the econom going again, and large numbers of blacks left the Sout and its poverty and chaos. But the vast majority had no choice but to remain.

There was a brief period of 'Reconstruction' when both blacks and whites tried to get together to create a more equal society, and some improvements were made, for example in school provision. But by 1877, when the victorious Federal troops were withdrawn, it was clear that 'Reconstruction' had failed and the North allowed the South to slip back into its old evil ways. The North made no attempt to support and protect the rights of the newly-freed slaves.

Some white people hated blacks so much they forme groups to attack and harm innocent black people. T Ku Klux Klan was one such organisation. Its membe wore white robes and rode armed in the night to att black people. They also attacked and burned the homes of those white people who had either befriended blacks, or who had formed unions with blac to fight for their rights. The Ku Klux Klan and other 'vigilante' groups frequently took the law into their own hands. They would tar and feather, rape and abuse, lynch and burn innocent people. It has been estimated that between 1865 and 1896 alone over 10,000 black men and women were lynched.

*A plantation owner with some of his workers. Mississippi, 1936.*

After the Civil War three additions were made to the American constitution: the Thirteenth Amendment abolished slavery forever; the Fourteenth Amendment gave full citizenship to black men (not women); the Fifteenth Amendment gave black men the right to vote. However, by 1900 black people in the South had lost these rights. Beginning with Mississippi, the Southern states passed laws robbing black men of the vote, and legalizing racial segregation. The laws were known as 'Jim Crow laws'.

By passing segregation laws the South could keep blacks and whites apart as much as was possible. There was separate housing, schools, churches, eating and drinking places, as well as separate public transport, sporting facilities, hospitals, prisons, orphanages, and even morgues and cemeteries. The facilities for black people were vastly inferior to those for whites, and conditions for blacks were almost as bad as they had been under slavery. The system that grew up in the South in the early decades of the 20th century was similar to the system of apartheid in South Africa today.

# Conditions in the South

**Most black people in the South worked on the land. They worked under arrangements which kept them poor.**

The blacks in the South were forced to take on the dirtiest and worst-paid jobs, such as building roads and railways, repairing and building up the river banks to control flooding, or working in the saw-mills and timber-yards. The majority however became farm tenants and share-croppers. This was the system which replaced the old slave plantations.

Instead of wages, croppers would work for a planter in return for a share of the cotton crop at harvest time. They would be given some acres of land on a plantation which they would regard as theirs, and the planter would provide housing, food, clothes, seed, and the tools needed to work the land. This may *sound* reasonable, but what normally happened was that the croppers became dependent on the planter, who provided all of the furnishings on credit, and who did all the money calculations. At the end of the year the croppers, after paying for their furnishings, were usually in debt to the landowner. Matters were really desperate if there was a bad crop.

Both blacks and whites became tenants and share-croppers. By the early 1930's, there were over 8.5 million people caught in the system, of whom a third were black. Working from dawn till dusk, they lived in wretched wooden cabins without sanitation or electricity, eating poorly, and drinking bad water. Disease was widespread, especially pellagra, malaria and ague. There were few medical facilities. Share-croppers, black and white, would raise large families, as each new child meant an extra pair of hands to dig, plough, chop weeds, or pick cotton.

*Photographs of a poor white family of sharecroppers in Alabama, taken in 1936.*

A group of black and white farm workers in 1936 who decided to unite in a trade union.

OCTOBER 25, 1929.

TWO CENTS

WORST STOCK CRASH STEMMED BY BANKS;
12,894,650-SHARE DAY SWAMPS MARKET;
LEADERS CONFER, FIND CONDITIONS SOUND

FINANCIERS EASE TENSION

Five Wall Street Bankers Hold Two Meetings at Morgan Office.

Wall Street Optimistic After Stormy Day; Clerical Work May Force Holiday Tomorrow

LOSSES RECOVERED

# The Depression

**A serious economic depression in America started in the 1920s. By 1931 poverty was widespread and unemployment rose as high as 13 million.**

*Roll of Thunder, Hear My Cry* is set in the 1930's during the time of the Depression. The South was hit very hard by the Depression. The price of cotton fell dramatically, and this was to create very serious hardship for the majority of people, both black and white. The arrival of the four-row cultivator tractor made things worse. One person and one tractor could do the job of eight people and eight mules.

The Government's 'New Deal' aimed to help those worst hit. They distributed relief in the form of money, food, clothing, and set up work-projects for the unemployed. Photographers were sent down to the South to produce evidence of poverty. (Many of the photos in this booklet were taken by these photographers.) However, those organising relief locally were usually white and went along with the local system. Black people were usually the last to receive relief and the first to be cut off from it. But poor people also began to organise and help themselves. It was very unusual in the South for black and white people to work together in this way, but extreme poverty and bad conditions brought them together. In the face of vicious opposition, some of them formed trade unions to fight for more money and better work conditions. The landlords and race-hate groups like the Ku Klux Klan used violence to try to break up the unions and terrorise their members. In 1936 one union organiser wrote:

**While violence of one type or another has been continually poured upon the membership of the Union...it was in March 1935 that a 'reign of terror' ripped into the country like a hurricane. For two-and-a-half months, violence raged through northeastern Arkansas and in neighbouring states...Meetings were banned and broken up; members were falsely accused, arrested and jailed, convicted on trumped up charges and thrown into prison; relief was shut off; union members were evicted from the land by the hundreds; homes were riddled with bullets from machine guns; churches were burned and school-houses stuffed with hay and floors removed; highways were patrolled night and day by armed vigilantes looking for the leaders; organisers were beaten, mobbed and murdered until the entire country was terrorized.**

*Mississippi Ferry, Vicksburg.*

# After the Second World War

**Many black people fought and died in the Second World War. They did so in the cause of freedom from tyranny. The experience of the war abroad changed attitudes in America.**

When America entered the Second World War in 1941 the government was forced to shelve its attempts to do something about the problems of poverty and the neglect of basic human rights at home. But when black soldiers returned after the war they were not prepared to settle for the way things had been in the past. Slowly a new movement grew: the movement for civil rights.

*Black GI's in the South Pacific during the Second World War.*

By the early 1950's the struggle of black people against segregation was forcing the American government to take action. In 1954, the Supreme Court declared that segregated schools were unconstitutional and ordered the Southern states to abolish them. The integration of Little Rock Central High School in Arkansas was one of the earliest and most famous cases. The State Governor, Orville Fanbus, decided to defy the Supreme Court order and called out the state troops to prevent nine black students from entering the school.

President Eisenhower was forced to use federal troops to ensure the safety of the black students as they entered the school. The students continued to attend school that year despite constant attacks and threats from white students. In autumn 1958 Governor Fanbus closed Central High School and three other Little Rock High Schools, rather than obey the Supreme Court order.

At about the same time, black people were protesting against the way in which buses in the South were still segregated. In 1955, in Montgomery, Alabama, a black woman, Rosa Parkes, was jailed for refusing to give up her seat to a white woman. Angry black people, led by Martin Luther King, decided to boycott the city's buses. They walked, rode mules hitched lifts, or shared cars – and the buses went empty. The boycott was successful – and in 1956 the Supreme Court declared that segregated buses were illegal.

*The Lincoln Memorial, Washington 1963.*

# The Civil Rights Movement grows

**During the 1960s the Civil Rights Movement grew stronger. Despite fierce opposition in the South, the movement achieved considerable success.**

In the early 1960s, large numbers of young black – and white – people went South to take part in further campaigns of non-violent direct action to challenge segregation. They took part in the registration of black voters, went on 'Freedom Rides' to desegregate buses and held sit-ins in restaurants which forced black customers to sit separately from whites.

*The Reverend Martin Luther King, Jr., addressing the 1963 Civil Rights March on Washington.*

In 1963, in the biggest demonstration the city had ever known, Civil Rights supporters marched on Washington. A quarter of a million people gathered at the Lincoln Memorial to hear Martin Luther King give a speech. Here is an extract from that famous speech.

**...I still have a dream. It is a dream deeply rooted in the American dream. I have a dream that one day this nation will rise up, live out the true meaning of its creed: 'We hold these truths to be self-evident, that all men are created equal.'**

**I have a dream that one day on the red hills of Georgia the sons of former slaves and the sons of former slave-owners will be able to sit down together at the table of brotherhood. I have a dream that one day even the state of Mississippi, a state sweltering with the heat of injustice, sweltering with the heat of oppression, will be transformed into an oasis of freedom and justice.**

**I have a dream that my four little children will one day live in a nation where they will not be judged by the color of their skin but by the content of their character...I have a Dream today...**

**Let freedom ring...and when this happens...when we allow freedom to ring – when we let it ring from every village and every hamlet, from every state and every city – we will be able to speed up that day when all of God's children – black men and white men, Jews and Gentiles, Protestants and Catholics – will be able to join hands and sing in the words of the old Negro spiritual, 'Free at last, free at last, Great God a-mighty, we are free at last!'**

*Martin Luther King*

Malcolm X.

*Angela Davis was active on behalf of black political prisoners. As a result, she was herself accused of crimes she did not commit.*

**WANTED BY THE FBI**

**INTERSTATE FLIGHT - MURDER, KIDNAPING**

**ANGELA YVONNE DAVIS**

FBI No. 867,615 G

Photograph taken 1969

Photograph taken 1970

**Alias:** "Tamu"

**DESCRIPTION**

| | | | |
|---|---|---|---|
| **Age:** | 26, born January 26, 1944, Birmingham, Alabama | | |
| **Height:** | 5'8" | **Eyes:** | Brown |
| **Weight:** | 145 pounds | **Complexion:** | Light brown |
| **Build:** | Slender | **Race:** | Negro |
| **Hair:** | Black | **Nationality:** | American |
| **Occupation:** | Teacher | | |
| **Scars and Marks:** | Small scars on both knees | | |

**Fingerprint Classification:** 4 M 5 Ua 6 / I 17 U

# The Struggle Continues

**After the death of Martin Luther King the style of the campaign for equal rights changed: some of its new leaders were more militant and many of its supporters were more more impatient.**

*Black athletes at the Mexico Olympics in 1968 giving a Black Power salute at the medal ceremony.*

The Civil Rights Movement was supported by millions of people throughout the United States. But many state governments were slow to respond with new laws and new policies – and powerful white groups were still opposed to what the Civil Rights Movement stood for.

Martin Luther King hoped that justice for all could be achieved by patient and peaceful means. But he himself was assassinated in 1968 – three years after another important black leader, Malcolm X, was killed. After their deaths a new style of campaign developed among groups known at the time as Black Power groups. Black Power groups identified closely with black people in Africa and, in some cases, with the Islamic religion. Their style was militant and aggressive: *demanding* equal rights, not just asking. They were considered dangerous by the white establishment and their leaders were subjected to constant police attention. Angela Davis, for example, was imprisoned – on trumped-up charges – for her activities.

The fear of the white establishment was heightened because, around this time, there were riots in many big cities in the United States. These riots showed anger and impatience that the demands for equal rights were still not being met.

Since these protests in the early 1970's there have been some changes in laws and policies. Black people have continued to organize themselves and to ally themselves with other oppressed groups in the United States, like Mexican-Americans, Puerto Ricans and American-Indians. The struggle for equal rights is not yet ended.

**Mildred Taylor was born in Mississippi. In this extract from an interview she explains how she came to write *Roll of Thunder, Hear My Cry.***

❛ From as far back as I can remember my father taught me a history different from the one I learned in school. By the fireside in our Ohio home and in Mississippi, where I was born and where my father's family had lived since the days of slavery, I had heard about our past. It was not an organized history beginning in a certain year, but one told through stories – stories about great-grandparents and aunts and uncles and others that stretched back through the years of slavery and beyond. It was a history of ordinary people, some brave, some not so brave, but basically people who had done nothing more spectacular than survive in a society designed for their destruction. Some of the stories my father had learned from his parents and grandparents as they had learned them from theirs; others he hold first-hand, having been involved in the incidents himself. There was often humor in his stories, sometimes pathos, and frequently tragedy; but always the people were graced with a simple dignity that elevated them from the ordinary to the heroic.

# THE AUTHOR

In *Roll of Thunder, Hear My Cry* I included the teachings of my own childhood, the values and principles by which I and so many other Black children were reared, for I wanted to show a different kind of Black world from the one so often seen. I wanted to show a family united in love and self-respect, and parents, strong and sensitive, attempting to guide their children successfully, without harming their spirits, through the hazardous maze of living in a discriminatory society.

I also wanted to show the Black person as heroic. In my own school days, a class devoted to the history of Black people in the United States always caused me painful embarrassment. This would not have been so if that history had been presented truly, showing the accomplishments of the Black race both in Africa and in this hemisphere. But as it was, the indictment of slavery was also an indictment of the people who were enslaved – a people who, according to the texts, were docile and childlike, accepting their fate without once attempting to free themselves. To me, this lackluster history of Black people totally devoid of any heroic or pride-building qualities was as much a condemnation of myself as it was of my ancestors and being the only Black child in an otherwise all-white class during my upper grade school years, I was acutely aware that that history did not measure up to the more romantic histories presented of other groups. I used to sit tensely waiting out those class hours trying to think of ways to repudiate what the textbooks said, for I recognized that there was a terrible contradiction between what was in them and what I had learned at home.

It is my hope that to the children who read my books, the Logans will provide the heroes missing from the schoolbooks of my childhood, Black men, women and children of whom they can be proud. ❜

**USE THIS PAGE AFTER**
**READING THE FIRST CHAPTER**

# THE FIRST CHAPTER

Read through these quotations from Chapter 1 and decide who said each one. Then fill in the chart below. In the second column, put the number of each statement next to the right person's name. In the third column, write down your first impressions of each character using not more than *three* words.

9. **'See, Miz Crocker, see what it says. They give us these ole books when they didn't want 'em no more.'**

2. **'Look out there, Cassie girl. All that belongs to you. You ain't never had to live on nobody's place but your own and as long as I live and the family survives, you'll never have to. That's important. You may not understand that now, but one day you will. Then you'll see.'**

10. **'I don't want my book neither.'**

7. **'And to all our little first grade friends only today starting on the road to knowledge and education, may your tiny feet find the pathways of learning steady and forever before you.'**

12b. **'Maybe so,' said ... 'but that doesn't mean they have to accept them ... and maybe we don't either.'**

1. **'Y'all go ahead and get dirty if y'all wanna ... Me, I'm gonna stay clean.'**

11. **'In the first place no-one cares enough to come down here, and in the second place if anyone should come, maybe he could see all the things we need - current books for all of our subjects, not just somebody's old throwaways, desks, paper, blackboards, erasers, maps, chalk ...'**

5. **'But I'll get my clothes dirty.'**

6. **'Y'all jus' startin' school today?'**
**'Yeah,' replied Stacey.**
**'I wishin' ours was jus' startin',' sighed ... 'Ours been goin' since the end of August.'**

12a. **Well, I just think you're spoiling those children, ... They've got to learn how things are sometime.'**

3b. **...'If that's what you think, you don't know Mama.'**

4. **'Well, since y'all don't seem to know nothin' ... maybe I ought not to tell y'all. It might hurt y'all's little ears.'**

3a. **'Look on the bright side,' said ... 'Jus' think of the advantage you've got. You'll be learnin' all sorts of stuff 'fore the rest of us ...' He smiled slyly. 'Like what's on all them tests.'**

8. **'I - I said may I have another book please, ma'am,' ... squeaked. 'That one's dirty.'**

| NAME | STATEMENT NUMBER | WHAT ARE THEY LIKE? |
|---|---|---|
| Cassie | | |
| Stacey | | |
| Little Man | | |
| Mama | | |
| Papa | | |
| Miss Crocker | | |
| T.J. | | |
| Jeremy | | |

If you only knew the first chapter of this book, what would you think it was going to be about? Here is a list of words. Choose the three which you think are going to be *most* important.

| | |
|---|---|
| share-cropping | school |
| punishment | family life |
| resistance | conflict |
| the land | money |
| friendship | clothes |
| growing up | food |
| transport | life in the countryside |
| books | fear |

*Roll of Thunder, Hear My Cry* is about the Logan family. One thing that everybody in that family knows about is their family tree.

Copy out the outline of the family tree below and use the information you find about the Logan's family history on pages 77-81 and 106-107 to complete it.

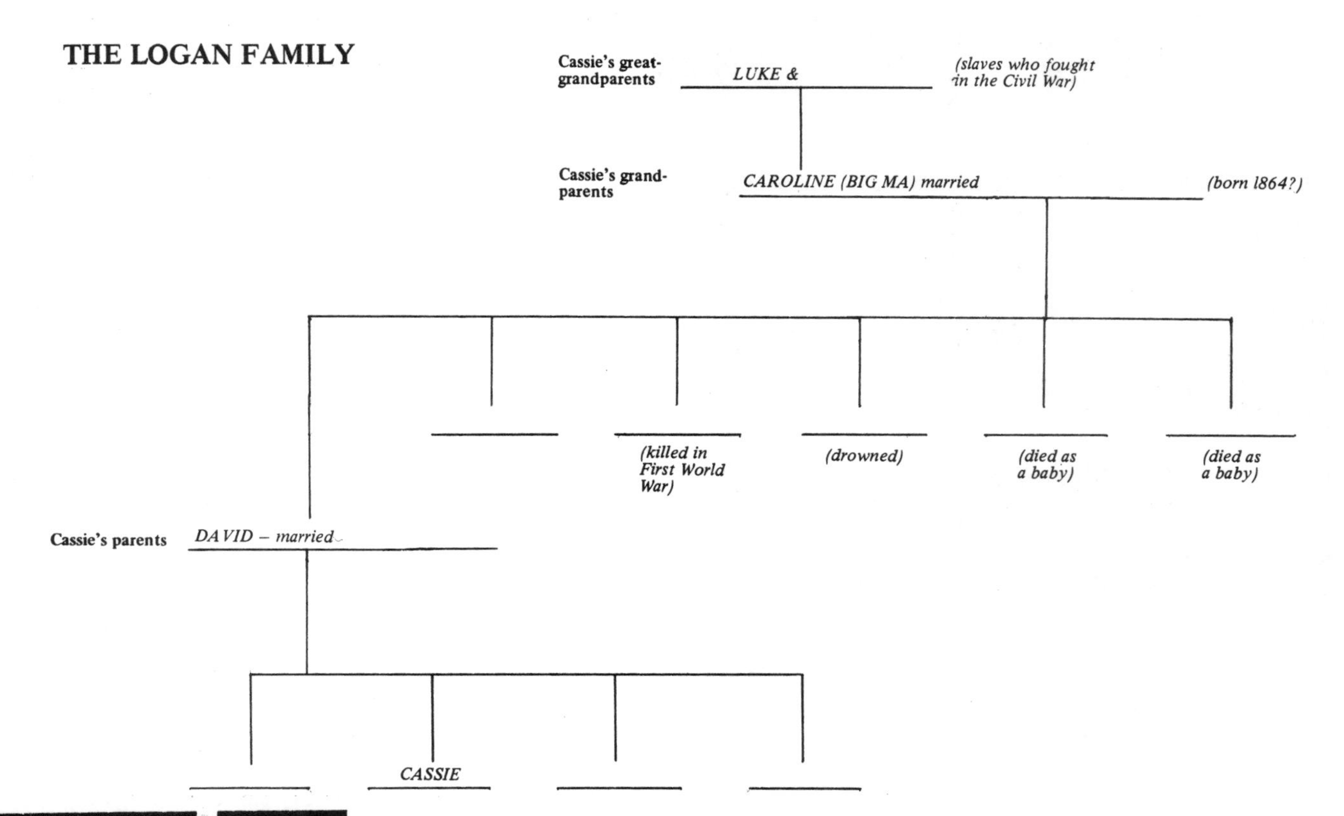

# FAMILIES

Other families in the book are important because of their relationship with the Logans.

Copy out the three charts below and fill in the necessary information.

**THE JAMISON FAMILY**

*CHARLES JAMISON & MRS JAMISON*

*(died 1918)*

*(sold Grandpa Logan 200 acres)*

**THE AVERY FAMILY**

*MR & MRS AVERY*

**THE SIMMS FAMILY**

*CHARLIE SIMMS*

# RACISM IN THE SOUTH: the 1930s

**In *Roll of Thunder, Hear My Cry,* Mildred Taylor writes about the experience of black people living in the South during the 1930s. In the following extracts Richard Wright and Billie Holiday write about their own experience at this time.**

## Learning rapidly

One of America's great black writers, Richard Wright, was brought up in the South and wrote about his childhood experiences in the novel *Black Boy*. He worked as a delivery boy for a general store.

**The store owned a bicycle which I used in delivering purchases. One day, while returning from the suburbs, my bicycle tyre was punctured. I walked along the hot, dusty road, sweating and leading the bicycle by the handle bars.
A car slowed at my side.
'What's the matter there, boy?' a white man called.
I told him that my bicycle was broken and that I was walking back to town.
'That's too bad,' he said. 'Hop on the running board.'
He stopped the car. I clutched hard at my bicycle with one hand and clung to the side of the car with the other.
'All set?'
'Yes, sir.'
The car started. It was full of young white men. They were drinking. I watched the flask pass from mouth to mouth.
'Wanna drink, boy?' one asked.
The memory of my six-year-old drinking came back and filled me with caution. But I laughed, the wind whipping my face.
'Oh, no!' I said.
The words were barely out of my mouth before I felt something hard and cold smash me between the eyes. It was an empty whisky bottle. I saw stars, and fell backwards from the speeding car into the dust of the road, my feet becoming entangled in the steel spokes of the bicycle. The car stopped and the white men piled out and stood over me.
'Nigger, ain't you learned no better sense'n that yet?' asked the man who hit me. 'Ain't you learned to say sir to a white man yet?'
Dazed, I pulled to my feet. My elbows and legs were bleeding. Fists doubled, the white man advanced, kicking the bicycle out of the way.
'Aw, leave the bastard alone. He's got enough,' said one.
They stood looking at me. I rubbed my shins, trying to stop the flow of blood. No doubt they felt a sort of contemptuous pity, for one asked:
'You wanna ride to town now, nigger? You reckon you know enough to ride now?'
'I wanna walk,' I said simply.
Maybe I sounded funny. They laughed.
'Well, walk, you black sonofabitch!'
Before they got back into their car, they comforted me with:
'Nigger, you sure ought to be glad it was us you talked to that way. You're a lucky bastard, 'cause if you'd said that to some other white man, you might've been a dead nigger now.'**

**I was learning rapidly how to watch white people, to observe their every move, every fleeting expression, how to interpret what was said and what left unsaid.**

*Black Boy,* Richard Wright

# Tired of scenes

Billie Holiday was one of the greatest jazz and blues singers to come out of America. She came from a very poor family and lived a full but hard and, in the end, sad life. She wrote a book about her musical life called *Lady Sings the Blues* and in one part she describes her experiences in the deep South touring with an all white orchestra led by Artie Shaw. The members of the band were, of course, her friends.

> **Most of the cats in the band were wonderful to me, but I got so tired of scenes in crummy roadside restaurants over getting served, I used to beg Georgie Auld, Tony Pastor, and Chuck Peterson to just let me sit in the bus and rest - and let them bring me out something in a sack. Some places they wouldn't even let me eat in the kitchen. Some places they would. Sometimes it was a choice between me eating and the whole band starving. I got tired of having a federal case over breakfast, lunch, and dinner.**
>
> **One time we stopped at a dirty little hole in the wall, and the whole band piled in. I was sitting at the counter next to Chuck Peterson. Everybody else gets waited on and this blonde bitch waitress ignores me like I'm not even there. Chuck called her first and then Tony Pastor got real sore. 'This is Lady Day.' He hollered at her, 'Now you feed her.'**
>
> **I pleaded with him not to start anything, but Tony let loose, the cats in the band started throwing things around. When they wouldn't serve me, the whole band pitched in and wrecked the joint. Everybody grabbed their food, and when the bus pulled out, you could hear the old sheriff's police-siren coming after us. Even Artie jumped into that fight.**

Later Billie Holiday describes how living under this kind of strain made her ill.

> **Eating was a mess, sleeping was a problem, but the biggest drag of all was a simple little thing like finding a place to go to the bathroom.**
>
> **Sometimes we'd make a six-hundred-mile jump and only stop once. Then it would be a place where I couldn't get served, let alone crash the toilet without causing a scene. At first I used to be so ashamed. Then finally I just said to hell with it. When I had to go I'd just ask the bus driver to stop and let me off at the side of the road. I'd rather go in the bushes than take a chance in the restaurants and towns.**
>
> **I kept doing this for so long, come rain and come shine, hot or cold, that it finally began to tell on me. The nervousness and strain finally fixed me so, I was good and sick.**

One of Billie Holiday's greatest recordings was the song 'Strange Fruit', which is a statement on the racism and brutality of the deep South. Here are the words:

> **Southern trees bear a strange fruit**<br>**Blood on the leaves and blood at the root**<br>**Black bodies swingin' in the Southern breeze**<br>**Strange fruit hangin' from the poplar trees**
>
> **Pastoral scene of the gallant South**<br>**The bulging eye and the twisted mouth**<br>**Scent of Magnolia sweet and fresh**<br>**Then the sudden smell of burning flesh**
>
> **Here is a fruit for the crows to pluck**<br>**For the rain to gather, for the wind to suck**<br>**For the sun to rot, for the tree to drop . . .**<br>**Here is a strange and bitter crop**

*Lady Sings the Blues,* Billie Holiday

# RACISM...

Throughout *Roll of Thunder, Hear My Cry* we are shown how black people are the victims of acts of violence and injustice similar to those described in the previous pages. These acts range from vicious murder to petty discrimination. Black people are constantly under threat.

The chart below is incomplete. The first column describes an act of violence or injustice. The second column gives the name of the person or people who suffer it. The third column says who is responsible for it. Complete the chart - and then add any more incidents you can think of within the story where black people are victimised.

| 1. ACTS OF VIOLENCE OR INJUSTICE | 2. WHO SUFFERS? | 3. WHO IS RESPONSIBLE? |
|---|---|---|
| Pupils are given tatty books | | The Board of Education |
| | Mr Berry and his nephews | |
| | | The bus driver |
| | Mary Logan | Kaleb Wallace & Harlan Granger |
| Attacked on the way back from Vicksburg | Mr Logan | |
| | T.J. | |
| | Cassie | Lillian Jean & Mrs Simms |

# RESISTANCE...

But black people in the story don't just accept these acts of violence and injustice: they try to find ways of resisting and fighting back. This is difficult and dangerous: they have to be careful and sometimes indirect in what they do.

Look back at the chart on the opposite page. Then, where you can, complete the last two columns below. The fourth column describes what black people in the story do to resist and fight back. The fifth column says what happens as a result of what they do. (You may decide that for some of the acts of violence or injustice on the chart there is nothing to put in these two columns.)

| 4. RESISTANCE OR REVENGE | 5. THE CONSEQUENCES |
|---|---|
| Little Man and Cassie refuse to take the books | |
| The Logan children dig a hole in the road | |

# REVENGE...

'Oh how sweet was well-manoeuvered revenge!'

There are two occasions in the book when Cassie and Stacey take their revenge when an injustice is done to them. The first is when Stacey sabotages the school bus. The second is when Cassie repays Lillian Jean for her humiliation in Strawberry.

## The bus

- He eyed us conspiratorily.
'I'll show y'all how we're gonna
'I'll show y'all how we're gonna stop that bus splashing us.'
'How? asked Little Man, eager for revenge.
'Don't have time to explain now. Just meet me. And on time. It's gonna take us all lunch hour.'

- He collapsed in silence by the door, breathing hard, and although I could not see him, I knew that his face was drawn and that his eyes had taken on a haggard look. I touched his arm lightly.
'Ain't no call to go blaming yourself', I said.
'We all done it.'
'But I got us into it', he said listlessly.

- 'Then it wasn't 'cause of the bus? Christopher-John blurted out...
'Well if anybody said them night men was down in here 'cause of some stupid bus, they crazy,' said T.J. authoritatively.

At first Stacey believes that his plan is foolproof. When the nightriders come he is terrified. It is not until he learns about their true purpose he begins to relax.

Write three entries in the diary that Stacey might have kept during this time. The first, directly after the successful destruction of the bus; the second, the day after the night riders have been; the third, two weeks later when he learns why they really came.

In the third entry try to include Stacey's feeling about what happens to Mr. Tatum.

## Lillian Jean

- 'This here's an important decision, Cassie, very important – I want you to understand that – but I think you can handle it. Now, you listen to me, and you listen good. This thing, if you make the wrong decision and Charlie Simms gets involved, then I get involved and there'll be trouble.'

- For the month of January I was Lillian Jean's slave and she thoroughly enjoyed it. She even took to waiting for me in the morning with Jeremy so that I could carry her books. When friends of hers walked with us, she bragged about her little colored friend and almost hugged herself with pleasure when I called her 'Miz Lillian Jean.'

- I started up the trail, feeling good about myself, when Lillian Jean asked, bewildered, 'But, Cassie, why? You was such a nice girl...' I stared at her astonished. Then I turned and left the forest, not wanting to believe that Lilian Jean didn't even realise it had all been just a game.

When Cassie talks to Papa about the event in Strawberry he says she must decide for herself but warns her of the consequences if anything goes wrong. She works out a plan and keeps it up for one month. Then privately so that no-one else will ever know, she takes her revenge.

Write three extracts in the diary that Cassie might have kept during this time. The first after she 'made up' with Lillian Jean; the second a couple of weeks later when things are going well; the third after she has humiliated Lillian Jean.

When you are writing these entries try to include how Cassie thinks she is coping with her father's words of warning.

# RISKS...

Although the black characters in the book want to fight back they have to be very careful not to risk even more serious danger. The two incidents described below illustrate this problem.

## The labels

Early in the book Miss Crocker goes to see Mary Logan to tell her that Little Man and Cassie refused to take their schoolbooks because of the labels inside. Both Miss Crocker and Mary Logan are black teachers of black pupils. Part of their conversation is given below.

**Miss Crocker, dismayed by Mama's seeming unconcern for the seriousness of the matter, thrust her shoulders back and began moving away from the desk. 'You understand that if they don't have those books to study from, I'll have to fail them in both reading and composition, since I plan to base all my lessons around -' She stopped abruptly and stared in amazement at Mama.**

**'Mary, what in the world are you doing?'**

**Mama did not answer. She had trimmed the paper to the size of the books and was now dipping a gray-looking glue from the brown bottle onto the inside cover of one of the books. Then she took the paper and placed it over the glue.**

**'Mary Logan, do you know what you're doing? That book belongs to the county. If somebody from the superintendent's office ever comes down here and sees that book, you'll be in real trouble.'**

**Mama laughed and picked up the other book. 'In the first place no one cares enough to come down here, and in the second place if anyone should come, maybe he could see all the things we need - current books for all of our subjects, not just somebody's old throwaways, desks, paper, black-boards, erasers, maps, chalk ... ' Her voice trailed off as she glued the second book.**

**'Biting the hand that feeds you. That's what you're doing, Mary Logan, biting the hand that feeds you.'**

**Again, Mama laughed. 'If that's the case Daisy, I don't think I need that little bit of food.' With the second book finished, she stared at a small pile of seventh-grade books on her desk.**

**'Well, I just think you're spoiling those children, Mary. They've got to learn how things are sometime.'**

**'Maybe so,' said Mama, 'but that doesn't mean they have to accept them ... and maybe we don't either.'**

In a short piece of writing try to explain the different attitudes the two women have - and then say who you think was right on this occasion.

## The sidewalk

When Uncle Hammer hears how Cassie was pushed off the sidewalk in Strawberry he is furious and storms off into the night armed with his shotgun. Mr.Morrison hurries after him to try to stop him.

Read the following statements carefully. From your knowledge of the characters, decide which statements might have been spoken by Uncle Hammer, and which by Mr Morrison:

**You'll be lynched.**

**The law ain't gonna help us so we gotta help ourselves.**

**You're as bad as they are if you act like that.**

**They'll think we're gutless.**

**Give them a taste of their own medicine.**

**They really need you.**

**Remember what happened to the Berrys.**

**What will happen to the family?**

**They're gonna push us around.**

**You think my brother died, and I got half my leg blown off in their German war to have some red-neck knock Cassie around anytime it suits him?**

**You'll just give them the excuse to take the land.**

Mr Morrison does succeed in bringing Hammer back, and as Stacey says:

**'Y'all better be glad nothin' happened ..... 'Cause I heard Big Ma tell Mama last night that if Mr Morrison didn't stop Uncle Hammer, Uncle Hammer might get killed.'**

Now write the conversation which you think took place when Mr Morrison persuades Uncle Hammer against revenge. You may prefer to write this in the form of a play.

# RACISM IN THE SOUTH: after the 1930s

**As *Roll of Thunder, Hear My Cry* shows, for black people in the 1930s the risks involved in every act of resistance were great. Even after the Second World War the situation did not greatly improve.**

## The 1940s: Dynamite Hill

In her autobiography, Angela Davis describes her experience of segregation during her childhood in the 1940s.

> **At the age of four I was aware that the people across the street were different - without yet being able to trace their alien nature to the color of their skin. What made them different from our neighbors in the projects was the frown on their faces, the way they stood a hundred feet away and glared at us, their refusal to speak when we said 'Good afternoon.' An elderly couple across the street, the Montees, sat on their porch all the time, their eyes heavy with belligerence.**
>
> **Almost immediately after we moved there the white people got together and decided on a border line between them and us. Center Street became the line of demarcation. Provided that we stayed on 'our' side of the line (the east side) they let it be known we would be left in peace. If we ever crossed over to their side, war would be declared. Guns were hidden in our house and vigilance was constant.**
>
> **Fifty or so yards from his hatred, we went about our daily lives. My mother, on leave from her teaching job, took care of my younger brother Benny, while waiting to give birth to another child, my sister Fania. My father drove his old orange van to the service station each morning after dropping me off at nursery school. It was next door to the Children's Home Hospital - an old wooden building where I was born and where, at two, I had my tonsils removed. I was fascinated by the people dressed in white and tried to spend more time at the hospital than at the nursery. I had made up my mind that I was going to be a doctor - a children's doctor.**
>
> **Shortly after we moved to the hill, white people began moving out of the neighborhood and black families were moving in, buying old houses and building new ones. A black minister and his wife, the Deyaberts, crossed into white territory.**
>
> **It was evening in the spring of 1949. I was in the bathroom washing my white shoelaces for Sunday school the next morning when an explosion a hundred times louder than the loudest, most frightening thunderclap I had ever heard shook our house. Medicine bottles fell off the shelves, shattering all around me. The floor seemed to slip away from my feet as I raced into the kitchen and my frightened mother's arms.**
>
> **Crowds of angry black people came up the hill and stood on 'our' side, staring at the bombed-out ruins of the Deyabert's house. Far into the night they spoke of death. But of their own fear they said nothing. Apparently it did not exist, for black families continued to move in. The bombings were such a constant response that soon our neighborhood became known as Dynamite Hill.**

*Angela Davis: An Autobiography*

## The 1950s: I was to learn

Mildred Taylor, in her speech accepting the Newbery Award for *Roll of Thunder, Hear My Cry*, described how, during the 1950's, her family would pay an annual visit to their old home in the South.

> **As a small child I loved the South. I used to look forward with eager anticipation to the yearly trips we took there when my father would pack the car and my mother would fry chicken, bake a cake and sweet-potato pies, stir up jugs of ice water and lemonade, and set them all in a basket on the back seat of the car between my sister and me. In my early years the trip was a marvellous adventure, a twenty-hour picnic that took us into another time, another world; down dusty red roads and across creaky wooden bridges into the rich farm country of Mississippi, where I was born.**
>
> **And life was good then. Running barefoot in the heat of the summer sun, my skin darkening to a soft, umber hue; chasing butterflies in the day, fireflies at night; riding an old mule named Jack and a beautiful mare named Lady; even picking a puff of cotton or two - there seemed no better world. And at night when neighboring relatives would gather to sit on the moonlit porch or by the heat of the fire, depending on the season, talk would turn to the old people, to friends and relatives who then seemed to have lived so long ago. As the storytellers spoke in animated voices and**

enlivened their stories with movements of great gusto, I used to sit transfixed, listening, totally engrossed. It was a magical time.

Yet even magical times must end.

I do not remember how old I was when the stories became more than tales of faraway people, but rather, reality. I do not remember when the twenty-hour picnic no longer was a picnic, the adventure no longer an adventure. I only remember that one summer I suddenly felt a climbing nausea as we crossed the Ohio River into Kentucky and was again admonished by my parents that my sister and I were now in the South and must remain quiet when we pulled into gas stations, that we must not ask to use the restrooms, that they would do all the talking.

That summer and the summers to come I grew to realize that the lovely baskets of food my mother always packed for the trips, she prepared because we could not eat in the restaurants; that the long overnight ride was because we could not sleep in the motels; that the jugs of water and lemonade were because we could not drink at the water fountains - at least not the fountains marked 'White Only,' which were usually newer and cleaner. I was to learn the fear of the police siren. I was to learn to hate the patrolmen who frisked my father and made him spread-eagle - all because of thirty-five miles per hour. I was to learn the terror of the back road and the long, long wait for morning while my father, exhausted from the drive, tried to sleep as my mother watched guard.

*Newbery Award Acceptance 1977,* Mildred D. Taylor

**During the 50s and 60s however, the Civil Rights Movement began to take root and there were many incidents of collective action against the illegal segregation that was still being enforced in the South. Racism was under attack, but still dominant.**

# A little bit nervous

Here is the account of Elizabeth Eckford, one of nine black students who tried to enter the all white Little Rock Central High School in 1957.

Before I left home Mother called us into the living-room. She said we should have a word of prayer. Then I caught the bus and got off a block from the school...

At the corner I tried to pass through the long line of guards around the school. One of the guards pointed across the street. So I pointed in the same direction and asked whether he meant for me to cross the street and walk down. He nodded 'yes'. So, I walked across the street conscious of the crowd that stood there, but they moved away from me.

For a moment all I could hear was the shuffling of their feet. Then someone shouted, 'Here she comes, get ready!' I moved away from the crowd on the sidewalk and into the street. If the mob came at me I could then cross back over so the guards could protect me.

*Elizabeth Eckford on her way to Little Rock Central High School.*

The crowd moved in closer and then began to follow me, calling me names. I still wasn't afraid. Just a little bit nervous. Then my knees started to shake all of a sudden and I wondered whether I could make it to the center entrance a block away. It was the longest block I ever walked in my whole life.

Just then the guards let some white students go through...I walked up to the guard who had let the white students in. He...didn't move. When I tried to squeeze past him, he raised his bayonet and then the other guards closed in and they raised their bayonets. The crowd...moved closer and closer. Somebody started yelling, 'Lynch her! Lynch her!'

I tried to see a friendly face somewhere in the mob – someone who maybe would help. I looked into the face of an old woman and it seemed a kind face, but when I looked at her again, she spat on me.

They came closer, shouting, 'No nigger bitch is going to get in our school. Get out of here!'

I turned back to the guards but their faces told me I wouldn't get help from them. Then I looked down the block and saw a bench at the bus stop. I thought, 'If I can only get there I will be safe.'

When I finally got there, I don't think I could have gone another step. I sat down and the mob crowded up and began shouting all over again. Someone hollered, 'Drag her over to this tree! Let's take care of the nigger.' Just then a white man sat down beside me, put his arm around me and patted my shoulder. He raised my chin and said, 'Don't let them see you cry.'

Then, a white lady – she was very nice – she came over to me on the bench. She spoke to me but I don't remember now what she said. She put me on the bus and sat next to me. She asked me my name and tried to talk to me but I don't think I answered...The next thing I remember I was standing in front of the School for the Blind, where Mother works...I ran upstairs, and...I kept running until I reached Mother's classroom.

Mother was standing at the window with her head bowed, but she must have sensed I was there because she turned around. She looked as if she had been crying, and I wanted to tell her I was all right. But I couldn't speak. She put her arms around me and I cried.

Elizabeth Eckford

**In the 60s black people were still being refused service in many buses and restaurants. But resistance continued to grow.**

# Impossible to hate sickness

The following extract describes a sit-in by four young women at a Woolworth's snack-bar near a college in Jackson, Mississippi.

Seconds before 11.15 we were occupying three seats at the previously segregated Woolworth's lunch counter. In the beginning the waitresses seemed to ignore us, as if they really didn't know what was going on. Our waitress walked past us a couple of times before she noticed we had started to write our own orders down and realized we wanted service. She asked us what we wanted. We began to read to her from our order slips. She told us that we would be served at the back counter, which was for Negroes.

'We would like to be served here,' I said.

The waitress started to repeat what she had said, then stopped in the middle of the sentence. She turned the lights out behind the counter, and she and the other waitresses almost ran to the back of the store, deserting all their white customers. I guess they thought that violence would start immediately after the whites at the counter realized what was going on. There were five or six other people at the counter. A couple of them just got up and walked away. A girl sitting next to me finished her banana split before leaving.

...At noon, students from a nearby white high school started pouring in to Woolworth's. When they first saw us they were sort of surprised. They didn't know how to react. A few started to heckle and the newsmen became interested again. Then the white students started chanting all kinds of anti-Negro slogans. We were called a little bit of everything. The rest of the seats except the three we were occupying had been roped off to prevent others from sitting down. A couple of the boys took one end of the rope and made it into a hangman's noose. Several attempts were made to put it around our necks. The crowds grew as more students and adults came in for lunch.

We kept our eyes straight forward and did not look at the crowd except for occasional glances to see what was going on.

...Memphis suggested that we pray. We bowed our heads, and all hell broke loose. A man rushed forward, threw Memphis from his seat, and slapped my face. Then another man who worked in the store threw me against an adjoining counter... I was dragged about thirty feet toward the door by my hair when someone made them turn me loose. As I was getting up off the floor, I saw Joan coming back inside. We started back to the center of the counter to join Pearlena. Lois Chaffee, a white Tougaloo faculty member, was now sitting next to her. So Joan and I just climbed across the rope at the front end of the counter and sat down. There were now four of us, two whites and two Negroes, all women. The mob started smearing us with ketchup, mustard, sugar, pies, and everything on the counter. Soon Joan and I were joined by John Salter, but the moment he sat down he was hit on the jaw with what appeared to be brass knuckles. Blood gushed from his face and someone threw salt into the open wound. Ed King, Tougaloo's chaplain, rushed to him.

We sat there for three hours taking a beating when the manager decided to close the store because the mob had begun to go wild with stuff from other counters. He begged and begged everyone to leave. But even after fifteen minutes of begging, no one budged. They would not leave until we did. Then Dr. Beittel, the president of Tougaloo College, came running in. He said he had just heard what was happening.

About ninety policemen were standing outside the store; they had been watching the whole thing through the windows, but had not come in to stop the mob or do anything. President Beittel went outside and asked Captain Ray to come and escort us out. The captain refused, stating the manager had to invite him in before he could enter the premises, so Dr. Beittel himself brought us out. He had told the police that they had better protect us after we were outside the store. When we got outside, the policemen formed a single line that blocked the mob from us. However, they were allowed to throw at us everything they had collected. Within ten minutes, we were picked up by Reverend King in his station wagon and taken to the NAACP headquarters on Lynch Street.

After the sit-in, all I could think of was how sick Mississippi whites were. They believed so much in the segregated Southern way of life, they would kill to preserve it. I sat there in the NAACP office and thought of how many times they had killed when this way of life was threatened. I knew that the killing had just begun. 'Many more will die before it is over with,' I thought. Before the sit-in, I had always hated the whites in Mississippi. Now I knew it was impossible for me to hate sickness.

*Coming of Age in Mississippi,* Anne Moody

# FAITH IN SCHOOL

In Britain today schooling is compulsory for everyone from the age of 5 to 16 for a minimum of 190 days a year. Schooling is also free: the state provides for it from money collected through rates and taxes.

It hasn't always been like that. 130 years ago in Britain the state did not provide free schools for everyone. If you wanted schooling you had to pay for it - unless you were lucky enough to have a school in your area run by a church. Even then you could only go if you had the time, if you didn't have to work at home in a factory or on the land. So very many working class children didn't get to go to school at all - and those that did didn't go for long. Anyway, the general idea was that working class children didn't need much - if any - education. In fact giving them education might be dangerous.

## Sneaking into school

The same was true in America. Except if you were black and lived in the slave states of the South. In that case it wasn't just rare to go to school: it was against the law. Some black people managed to get some kind of education despite it all: at home; at church; from the few books that might be around. And, sometimes, at small illegal schools. In the extract below, Susie King Taylor describes her schooling in the town of Savannah in the state of Georgia 150 years ago.

**I was born under the slave law in Georgia in 1848 and was brought up by my grandmother in Savannah. There were three of us with her, my younger sister and brother. My brother and I being the two eldest, we were sent to a friend of my grandmother, a Mrs. Woodhouse, a widow, to learn to read and write. She was a free woman and lived on Bay Lane between Habersham and Price Streets, about half a mile from my house. We went every day with our books wrapped in paper to prevent the police or white persons from seeing them. We went in, one at a time, through the gate into the yard to the kitchen, which was the school room. She had 25 or 30 children whom she taught, assisted by her daughter, Mary Jane. The neighbors would see us going in some times, but they supposed we were there learning trades, as it was the custom to give children a trade of some kind. After school. we left the same way we entered, one by one and we would go to a square about a block from the school and wait for each other. We would gather laurel leaves and pop them in our hands, on our way home. I remained at her school for two years or more, when I was sent to a Mrs. Mary Beasley, where I continued until May 1860, when she told my grandmother she had taught me all she knew, and grandmother had better get someone else who could teach me more, so I stopped my studies for a while.**

*Reminiscences of My Life,* Susie King Taylor

## On a garbage dump

*Mary McLeod Bethune in later years.*

After slavery was abolished in America in 1866 it became legal for black children to go to school - but not, in the South, for them to go with white pupils. It took years and years before schools for black children became common; and always they were paid for directly by the people themselves - often through church collections - and not by the state. Getting a school started and keeping it going meant sacrifice and hard work. Here Mary McLeod Bethune describes how she started a school in the early years of this century, forty years after slavery ended.

**On October 3, 1904, I opened the doors of my school, with an enrollment of five little girls, aged from eight to twelve, whose parents paid me fifty cents' weekly tuition. My own child was the only boy in the school. Though I hadn't a penny left, I considered cash money as the smallest part of my resources. I had faith in a living God, faith in myself, and a desire to serve . . .**

A small country school, Alabama 1936.

We burned logs and used the charred splinters as pencils, and mashed elderberries for ink. I begged strangers for a broom, a lamp, a bit of cretonne to put around the packing case which served as my desk. I haunted the city dump and the trash piles behind hotels, retrieving discarded linen and kitchenware, cracked dishes, broken chairs, pieces of old lumber. Everything was scoured and mended. This was part of the training to salvage, to reconstruct, to make bricks without straw. As parents gradually began to leave their children overnight, I had to provide sleeping accommodations. I took corn sacks for mattresses. Then I picked Spanish moss from trees, dried and cured it, and used it as a substitute for mattress hair.

The school expanded fast. In less than two years I had 250 pupils. In desperation I hired a large hall next to my original little cottage, and used it as a combined dormitory and classroom. I concentrated more and more on girls, as I felt that they especially were hampered by lack of educational opportunities . . .

I had many volunteer workers and a few regular teachers, who were paid from fifteen to twenty-five dollars a month and board. I was supposed to keep the balance of the funds for my own pocket, but there was never any balance - only a yawning hole. I wore old clothes sent me by mission boards, recut and redesigned for me in our dress-making classes. At last I saw that our only solution was to stop renting space, and to buy and build our own college.

Near by was a field, popularly called Hell's Hole, which was used as a dumping ground. I approached the owner, determined to buy it. The price was $250. In a daze, he finally agreed to take five dollars down, and the balance in two years. I promised to be back in a few days with the initial payment. He never knew it, but I didn't have five dollars. I raised this sum selling ice cream and sweet-potato pies to the workmen on construction jobs, and I took the owner his money in small change wrapped in my handkerchief.

That's how the Bethune-Cookman college campus started.

Mary McLeod Bethune

# Into the fight

Most of the schools for black children, which had been created and kept going by so much effort, were eventually taken over by local government as part of the state-run school system. But in the South, schools - like everything else - stayed racially segregated. And schools for black children were, in comparison with schools for white children, over-crowded and poorly equipped. The teachers who taught in them were also paid much less. Things improved slightly in the 1920's - only because people fought for improvements themselves. In a city called Charleston (in North Carolina), for example, it wasn't until 1920 that *black* teachers could get jobs in schools for *black* children which the city council helped to finance. A black teacher called Paul Miller tried to get the law changed by a petition. Septima Clark, another black teacher, joined in.

That's when I got into the fight. I volunteered to seek signatures and started visiting the grass roots people. I worked Cannon Street, a very long street, from Rutledge all the way to King. Soon we brought in a tow sack - we called it a croaker sack, I remember, back in those days - with more than 10,000 signatures to the petition. I remember the number because of the fact that a white legislator known then as One-Eye Tillman had declared Mr Miller would never be able to get 10,000 signatures in all Charleston.

The law was passed. The next year, 1920, we had Negro teachers in the public schools of Charleston and the year following we had Negro principals. We had been victorious in this my first effort to establish for Negro citizens what I sincerely believed was no more than their God-given rights . . . .

*Echo in My Soul,* Septima Clark

# GREAT FAITH

By the 1930's the situation was better, but not that much better since Susie King Taylor had to break the law to learn to read and write. There are two schools in *Roll of Thunder, Hear My Cry*. One is the Jefferson Davis County School - which is for white pupils. The other is Great Faith Elementary and Secondary School - which is for black pupils.

Look at the statements below and decide which of them are *true* about *Great Faith School* according to the information in the book. (You will find pages 18-21, 30 and 41 useful for checking the statements.)

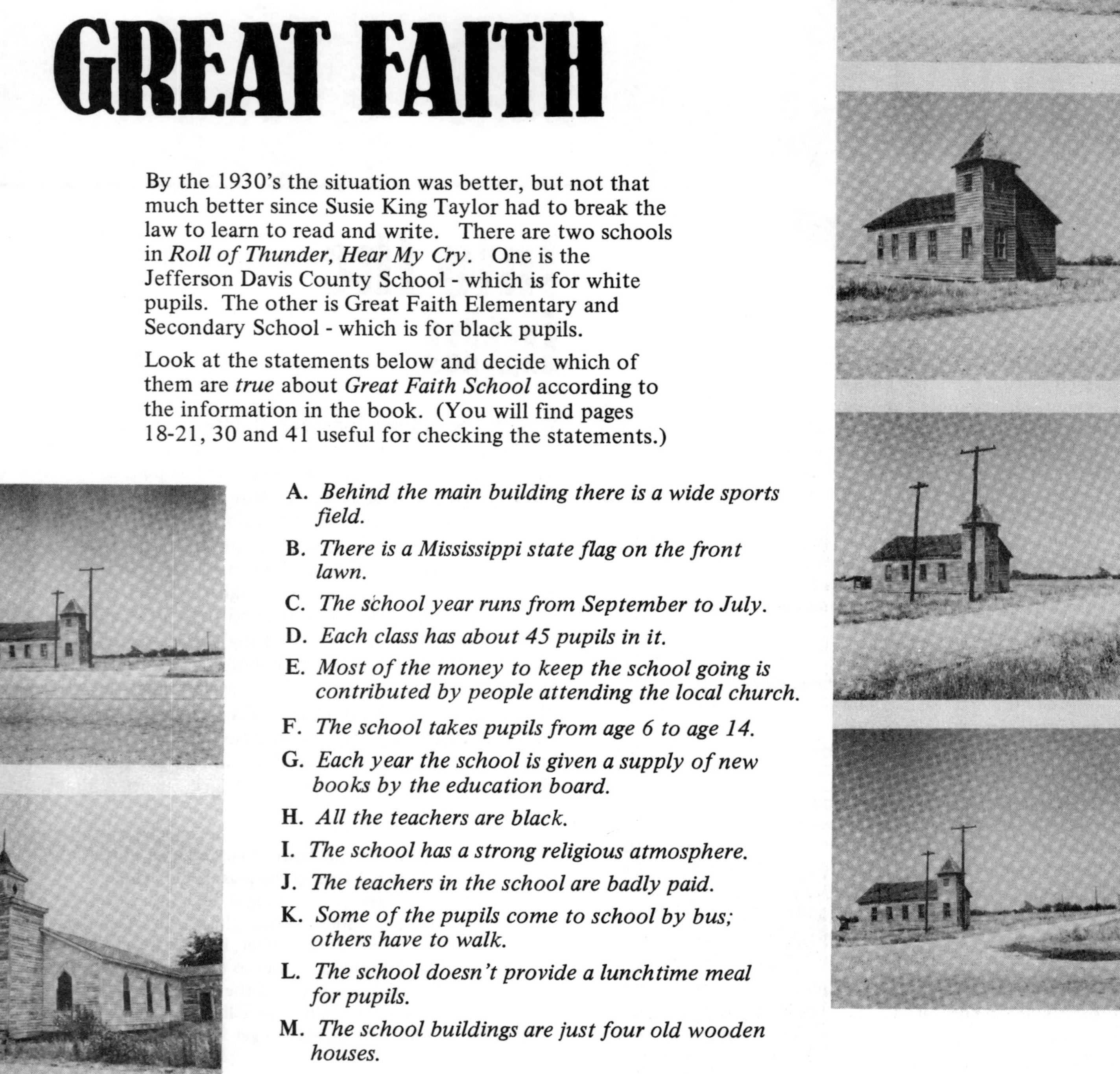

A. *Behind the main building there is a wide sports field.*

B. *There is a Mississippi state flag on the front lawn.*

C. *The school year runs from September to July.*

D. *Each class has about 45 pupils in it.*

E. *Most of the money to keep the school going is contributed by people attending the local church.*

F. *The school takes pupils from age 6 to age 14.*

G. *Each year the school is given a supply of new books by the education board.*

H. *All the teachers are black.*

I. *The school has a strong religious atmosphere.*

J. *The teachers in the school are badly paid.*

K. *Some of the pupils come to school by bus; others have to walk.*

L. *The school doesn't provide a lunchtime meal for pupils.*

M. *The school buildings are just four old wooden houses.*

N. *The teachers are only interested in teaching pupils to read and write.*

O. *There are strict uniform regulations at the school.*

P. *Most of the pupils at the school aren't bothered about getting an education.*

**FOR WRITING**

## 1. A SPEECH TO STUDENT TEACHERS

Education is very important to Mary Logan - as it is for other black characters in *Roll of Thunder, Hear My Cry*. As a teacher Mary Logan is paid very little and risks being fired if she steps out of line: but she believes in doing her job well.

Suppose that Mary Logan was asked to give a school speech to black students in a college which trains them to become teachers. What do you think she would say to them about the job of teaching in black schools? Put yourself into her 'voice' and write out the speech that she might give. Call it 'Being a teacher'.

If you like you could use in the speech *some* of the information given earlier in this section about the history of schools for black people. You could also refer to the conditions under which Mary Logan and her pupils have to work at Great Faith.

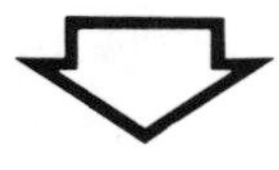

## 2. WALKING TO SCHOOL

Moe, one of Stacey's friends, does a 3½ hour walk each way to get to school at Great Faith. He too believes in school!

See if you can work out a poem which starts with Moe but goes on to say something about what school means to you. (Does it mean the same?)

# CASSIE & PAPA

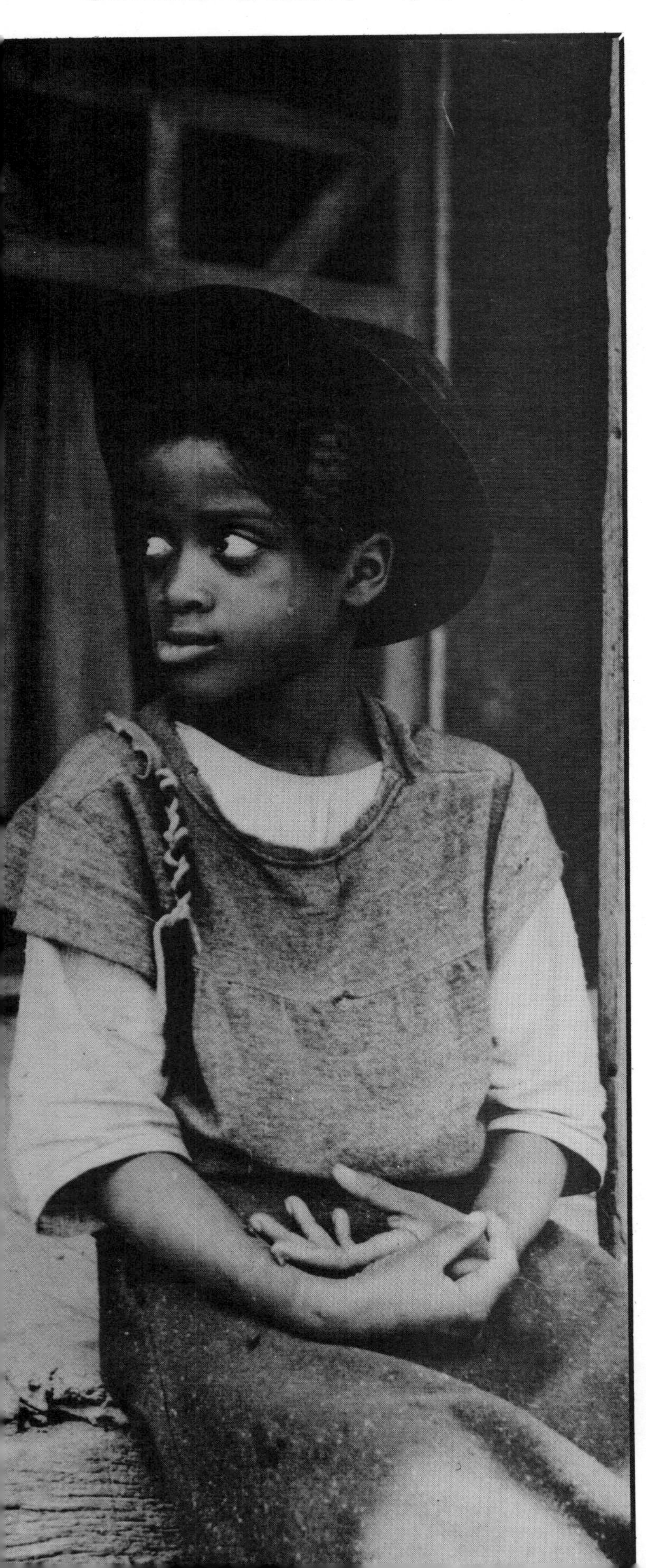

'To the memory of my beloved father who lived many adventures of the boy Stacey and who was in essence the man David.'

Mildred Taylor dedicated *Roll of Thunder, Hear My Cry* to her father. In the Author's Note to the book she explains his part in her life and her writing.

Cassie is influenced and guided by her father in the same way. Here are two things he says to her.

> **'Cassie, there'll be a whole lot of things you ain't gonna wanna do but you'll have to do in this life just so you can survive. You have to demand respect in this world, ain't nobody just gonna hand it to you. How you carry yourself, what you stand for – that's how you gain respect. But, little one, ain't nobody's respect worth more than your own.'**
> *page 143*

> **'You see that fig tree over yonder, Cassie? Them other trees all around...that oak and walnut, they're a lot bigger and they take up more room and give so much shade they almost overshadow that little ole fig. But that fig tree's got roots that run deep, and it belongs in that yard as much as that oak and walnut. It keeps on blooming, bearing good fruit year after year, knowing all the time it'll never get as big as them other trees. Just keeps on growing and doing what it gotta do. It don't give up. It give up, it'll die. There's a lesson to be learned from that little tree, Cassie girl, 'cause we're like it. We keep doing what we gotta, and we don't give up. We can't.'**
> *page 166*

There are some other pages where you can find some more examples:

page 12 – the family land
pages 38-39 – the bad influence of the Wallaces
page 122 – the importance of knowing about your own history
pages 129-130 – Stacey's friendship with Jeremy
page 219 – what is going to happen to T.J.

**FOR WRITING**

Using three or four examples from the book, write about the ways in which David Logan influences and guides Cassie – and his other children.

You might like to write two paragraphs on each example:
David Logan tells Cassie that...
From this she learns...

# JEREMY

When Jeremy first appears in the novel he is described as 'a towheaded boy, barefooted and pale'.

The following words are often used to describe him: shy, timid, quiet, awkward, hesitant.

We also find out that he is ridiculed by other white children and beaten by his father.

He seems to be an important character even though he does not appear very often:

- He tries to meet the Logan children on their way to school. (pp17-18, 158-159)
- He attempts to stick up for Cassie when his father demands an apology from her in Strawberry. (p19)
- He visits the Logans on Christmas Day with a special present for Stacey. (pp127-130)
- He meets the children in the forest when he can. (pp182-4)
- He brings news to Cassie, Christopher-John and Little Man about what is happening during the fire. (pp211-212)

The Logan children are the only people he confides in.

**JEREMY . . .**

**● 'Lillian Jean and R.W. and Melvin, I guess I don't like them very much.'**

**● 'Come these hot nights, I just climbs in my tree and it's like going into another world...**

**I think when I grow up I'm gonna build me a house in some trees and jus' live there all the time...'**

**IDEAS FOR WRITING**

Based on the information you can find about Jeremy, discuss why you think he has become the sort of boy he is and why Mildred Taylor decided to include such a character in her novel.

Afterwards you could use the points raised by your discussion to do a short piece of writing about Jeremy and his role in the novel.

It is now 1946 and Jeremy is a man of 25.

*Either*: Imagine that he is telling a friend about his childhood memories, in particular what happened between October 1933 and August 1934, and write an account of what he says.

*Or*: Think about some of the things Jeremy might have done since he was 12. Consider the following questions:

- Did he keep trying to win Stacey's friendship?
- Did he remain in the same area or move away?
- Did he become involved in the fight to bring the share-croppers together?

Now pick one particular thing that might have happened to Jeremy and write a story about it.

In *Let the Circle Be Unbroken*, the sequel to *Roll of Thunder, Hear My Cry* Mildred Taylor writes about what took place at TJ's trial. Although Cassie, Stacey, Christopher John and Little Man had been forbidden to go to the trial, they managed to see what went on by perching in the trees which overlooked the court room.

Below are the statements given by the two key witnesses in the trial and the facts established by Mr Jamison in his cross-examination. They have been adapted from chapter three of *Let the Circle Be Unbroken.* Read and compare them carefully and then choose one of the suggestions for writing.

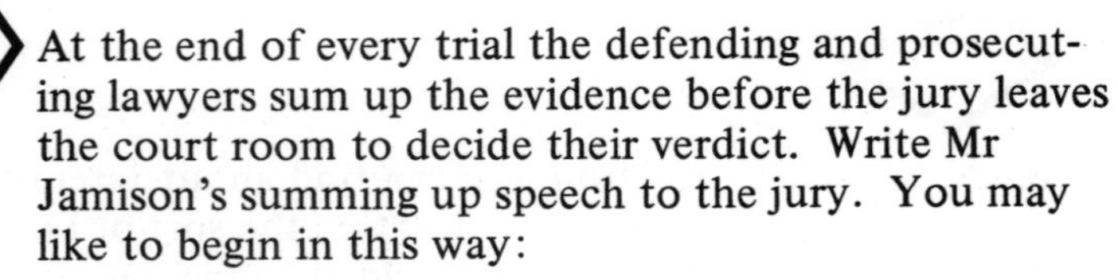


### FOR WRITING

At the end of every trial the defending and prosecuting lawyers sum up the evidence before the jury leaves the court room to decide their verdict. Write Mr Jamison's summing up speech to the jury. You may like to begin in this way:

*'Gentlemen of the jury, you have heard the testimonies of all the witnesses involved. It is now my job to summarise their evidence so that you can best decide if the defendant T.J. Avery is, beyond a shadow of a doubt, guilty as charged . . .'*

Write an account of what actually took place while Mr Jamison was examining one of the witnesses. You may like to write this in the form of a play.

As if you were writing a short part of a chapter in the book, describe Cassie's reactions to the verdict given by the jury. In *Let the Circle Be Unbroken* Mildred Taylor describes the verdict:

> **In less than thirty minutes the jury returned. The vote poll was taken. Twelve men on the jury. Twelve votes of guilty. There was to be no mercy.**
>
> **T.J. received the death penalty.**

Use the information you have gathered about the trial to write a newspaper report for the next edition of the *Strawberry Gazette*. Remember who the paper will be owned by and the point of view it will represent.

Here are some page references for the book that may help you with your piece of writing:

pages 159, 160, 167-168, 192, 196-198, 219-220.

### FACTS ESTABLISHED BY MR JAMISON IN RELATION TO MRS BARNETT'S STATEMENT

- The light switch at the top of the stairs leading down to the store wasn't working.
- The light in the store wasn't on.
- Mr Barnett was carrying a flashlight which remained on when he was knocked unconscious.
- Mrs Barnett wasn't wearing her glasses; she was near-sighted.
- When Mr and Mrs Barnett first saw the men they were twenty feet away.
- Two of the men were standing by the safe and the other was standing by the pistol case and didn't come near Mrs Barnett or her husband.
- Mrs Barnett could see that the men were black. She couldn't identify any facial features but she could tell that the two who attacked her husband were about the same height as him, 5 feet 10 inches.
- Mrs Barnett admitted that TJ was much smaller than 5'6".
- There were two black stockings found in the rubbish bin outside the store the day after Mr Barnett was murdered.
- There were two black stockings found in the rubbish bin outside the store the day after Mr Barnett was murdered. They didn't belong to Mrs Barnett because she had only bought black stockings to go into mourning after her husband's death.
- Mrs Barnett admitted she could not be sure that the two men who attacked her husband weren't wearing black stockings.

### MRS BARNETT'S STATEMENT

*On Sunday 25th August my husband Jim Lee Barnett and I went to our living quarters above the Mercantile shortly after six o'clock in the evening. We had supper and retired about eight o'clock. About an hour later we were awakened by noises from below. I followed Mr Barnett downstairs to investigate. We found three Negroes in the store and the safe door open. Mr Barnett attacked one of the Negroes and while they were fighting a second Negro hit him on the back of his head with the blunt end of an axe. I flew at them but they knocked me down and I must have become unconscious. When I came round the three were gone. My husband was still unconscious and bleeding badly from the wound on his head. Immediately I ran outside and started screaming for help.*

*Photographs of Vicksburg, 1936.*

**R.W. SIMMS' STATEMENT**

*That Sunday evening me and Melvin seen TJ walking in the direction of the nigra church. We was passing that way so we gave him a ride. While he was there him and a few nigra younguns fell out. He didn't want to stay so we give him a ride back to the front of our place and he walked off. We never said anything 'bout going to Strawberry with him or any old pearl-handled pistol.*

*We went into our place for about an hour then we took the truck into Strawberry 'cause we felt this urge to play pool. I don't know what time we arrived but it was late. We parked the truck and went in to play some pool. We was playing when we heard Mrs Barnett hollering for help. We all ran out and Melvin and me saw TJ and two other nigras running from the back of the Barnett. We spoke to TJ and he said he'd been playing cards in Ike Foster's shed and got caught cheating so he was running off. Then we went inside and seen what they done.*

**FACTS ESTABLISHED BY MR JAMISON IN RELATION TO R.W. SIMMS' STATEMENT**

- Mr Macabee, a local farmer, testified that he had picked TJ up shortly after nine o'clock on Soldier's Road and that he had been beaten up.
- Reverend Gabson, minister at the Great Faith Church, testified that he had overheard Mr RW and Mr Melvin talking to TJ about going into Strawberry to get a pearl handled pistol. He also stated that TJ had not been beaten up at that time, approximately seven o'clock.
- RW agreed that by the time they had dropped TJ outside his house, spent an hour inside and then driven to Strawberry, it must have been about nine o'clock before they arrived to play pool.
- RW agreed that his truck was easily recognisable because it had different coloured fenders.
- Mr Justice Overton, a respected member of the white community, testified that he had seen RW and Melvin's truck parked near the Barnett Mercantile on the night of the 25th at a few minutes past eight o'clock.

# SAME TIME, SAME PLACE, SAME STORY?

**In this section there are extracts from two novels. One is from *Roll of Thunder, Hear My Cry*. The other is from *To Kill a Mockingbird.***

## To Kill a Mockingbird

*To Kill a Mockingbird* was written by a white woman called Harper Lee. The story takes place in a fictitious town called Maycomb in the period 1932-1935. 'Maycomb' is very like Monroeville in Alabama (the next state to Mississippi – see map in this booklet) where Harper Lee grew up. It seems likely that the story of *To Kill a Mockingbird* was loosely based on events in Harper Lee's own childhood.

The story is told through the eyes of Scout, who is about 9 when the story ends. Jem, her brother, is four years older. The main part of the story concerns what happens when their father Atticus, who is a lawyer, decides to defend a black man called Tom Robinson against a charge of raping a white girl – a crime of which he is innocent.

Before his trial Tom Robinson is kept in the county jail and Atticus, fearing that a mob might attack the jail, decides to sit outside it overnight. Scout and Jem (with their friend Dill) follow him to see what is happening.

**As we walked up the sidewalk, we saw a solitary light burning in the distance. 'That's funny,' said Jem, 'jail doesn't have an outside light.'**

**'Looks like it's over the door,' said Dill.**

**A long extension cord ran between the bars of a second-floor window and down the side of the building. In the light from its bare bulb, Atticus was sitting propped against the front door. He was sitting in one of his office chairs, and he was reading, oblivious of the night-bugs dancing over his head.**

**I made to run, but Jem caught me. 'Don't go to him,' he said, 'he might not like it. He's all right, let's go home. I just wanted to see where he was.'**

**We were taking a short cut across the square when four dusty cars came in from the Meridian highway, moving slowly in a line. They went around the square, passed the bank building, and stopped in front of the jail.**

**Nobody got out. We saw Atticus look up from his newspaper. He closed it, folded it deliberately, dropped it in his lap, and pushed his hat to the back of his head. He seemed to be expecting them.**

**'Come on,' whispered Jem. We streaked across the square, across the street, until we were in the shelter of the Jitney Jungle door. Jem peeked up the sidewalk. 'We can get closer,' he said. He ran to Tyndal's Hardware door – near enough, at the same time discreet.**

**In ones and twos, men got out of the cars. Shadows became substance as light revealed solid shapes moving towards the jail door. Atticus remained where he was. The men hid him from view.**

**'He in there, Mr Finch?' a man said.**
**'He is,' we heard Atticus answer, 'and he's asleep. Don't wake him up.'**

**In obedience to my father, there followed what I later realized was a sickeningly comic aspect of an unfunny situation: the men talked in near-whispers.**

**'You know what we want,' another man said. 'Get aside from the door, Mr Finch.'**

**'You can turn around and go home again, Walter,' Atticus said pleasantly. 'Heck Tate's around somewhere.'**

**'The hell he is,' said another man. 'Heck's bunch's so deep in the woods they won't get out till mornin'.'**

**'Indeed? Why so?'**

**'Called 'em off on a snipe hunt,' was the succinct answer.***
**'Didn't you think a'that, Mr Finch?'**

**'Thought about it, but didn't believe it. Well then,' my father's voice was still the same, 'that changes things, doesn't it?'**

**'It do,' another deep voice said. Its owner was a shadow.**

**'Do you really think so?**

**This was the second time I heard Atticus ask that question in two days, and it meant somebody's man would get jumped. This was too good to miss. I broke away from Jem and ran as fast as I could to Atticus.**

***snipe hunt:** snipes are birds which live on marshes or river banks

Jem shrieked and tried to catch me, but I had a lead on him and Dill. I pushed my way through dark smelly bodies and burst into the circle of light.

'H-ey, Atticus!'

I thought he would have a fine surprise, but his face killed my joy. A flash of plain fear was going out of his eyes, but returned when Dill and Jem wriggled into the light.

There was a smell of stale whisky and pig-pen about, and when I glanced around I discovered that these men were strangers. They were not the people I saw last night. Hot embarrassment shot through me: I had leaped triumphantly into a ring of people I had never seen before.

Atticus got up from his chair, but he was moving slowly, like an old man. He put the newspaper down very carefully, adjusting its creases with lingering fingers. They were trembling a little.

'Go home, Jem,' he said. 'Take Scout and Dill home.'

We were accustomed to prompt, if not always cheerful acquiescence to Atticus's instructions, but from the way he stood Jem was not thinking of budging.

'Go home, I said.'

Jem shook his head. As Atticus's fists went to his hips, so did Jem's, and as they faced each other I could see little resemblance between them: Jem's soft brown hair and eyes, his oval face and snug-fitting ears were our mother's, contrasting oddly with Atticus's greying black hair and square-cut features, but they were somehow alike. Mutual defiance made them alike.

'Son, I said go home.'

Jem shook his head.

'I'll send him home,' a burly man said, and grabbed Jem roughly by the collar. He yanked Jem nearly off his feet.

'Don't you touch him!' I kicked the man swiftly. Barefooted, I was surprised to see him fall back in real pain. I intended to kick his shin, but aimed too high.

'That'll do, Scout.' Atticus put his hand on my shoulder. 'Don't kick folks. No –' he said, as I was pleading justification.

'Ain't nobody gonna do Jem that way,' I said.

'All right, Mr Finch, get 'em outa here,' someone growled. 'You got fifteen seconds to get 'em outa here.'

In the midst of this strange assembly, Atticus stood trying to make Jem mind him. 'I ain't going,' was his steady answer to Atticus's threats, requests, and finally, 'Please Jem, take them home.'

I was getting a bit tired of that, but felt Jem had his own reasons for doing as he did, in view of his prospects once Atticus did get him home. I looked around the crowd. It was a summer's night, but the men were dressed, most of them, in overalls and denim shirts buttoned up to the collars. I thought they must be cold-natured, as their sleeves were unrolled and buttoned at the cuffs. Some wore hats pulled firmly down over their ears. They were sullen-looking, sleepy-eyed men who seemed unused to late hours. I sought once more for a familiar face, and at the centre of the semicircle I found one.

'Hey, Mr Cunningham.'

The man did not hear me, it seemed.

'Hey, Mr Cunningham. How's your entailment gettin' along?'*

Mr Walter Cunningham's legal affairs were well known to me; Atticus had once described them at length. The big man blinked and hooked his thumbs in his overall straps. He seemed uncomfortable; he cleared his throat and looked away. My friendly overture had fallen flat.

Mr Cunningham wore no hat, and the top half of his forehead was white in contrast to his sun-scorched face, which led me to believe that he wore one most days. He shifted his feet, clad in heavy work shoes.

'Don't you remember me, Mr Cunningham? I'm Jean Louise Finch. You brought us some hickory nuts one time, remember?' I began to sense the futility one feels when unacknowledged by a chance acquaintance.

'I go to school with Walter,' I began again. 'He's your boy, ain't he? Ain't he, sir?'

Mr Cunningham was moved to a faint nod. He did know me, after all.

'He's in my grade,' I said, 'and he does right well. He's a good boy,' I added, 'a real nice boy. We brought him home for dinner one time. Maybe he told you about me, I beat him up one time but he was real nice about it. Tell him hey for me, won't you?'

*entailment: laws which restrict who inherits property.

From the film *To Kill a Mockingbird*

Atticus had said it was the polite thing to talk to people about what they were interested in, not about what you were interested in. Mr Cunningham displayed no interest in his son, so I tackled his entailment once more in a last-ditch effort to make him feel at home.

'Entailments are bad,' I was advising him, when I slowly awoke to the fact that I was addressing the entire aggregation. The men were all looking at me, some had their mouths half-open. Atticus had stopped poking at Jem; they were standing together beside Dill. Their attention amounted to fascination. Atticus's mouth, even, was half-open, an attitude he had once described as uncouth. Our eyes met and he shut it.

'Well, Atticus, I was just sayin' to Mr Cunningham that entailments are bad an' all that, but you said not to worry, it takes a long time sometimes...that you all'd ride it out together...' I was slowly drying up, wondering what idiocy I had committed. Entailments seemed all right enough for living-room talk.

I began to feel sweat gathering at the edges of my hair; I could stand anything but a bunch of people looking at me. They were quite still.

'What's the matter?' I asked.

Atticus said nothing. I looked around and up at Mr Cunningham, whose face was equally impassive. Then he did a peculiar thing. He squatted down and took me by both shoulders.

'I'll tell him you said hey, little lady,' he said.

Then he straightened up and waved a big paw. 'Let's clear out,' he called. 'Let's get going, boys.'

As they had come in, in ones and twos the men shuffled back to their ramshackle cars. Doors slammed, engines coughed, and they were gone.

I turned to Atticus, but Atticus had gone to the jail and was leaning against it with his face to the wall. I went to him and pulled his sleeve. 'Can we go home now?' He nodded, produced his handkerchief, gave his face a going-over and blew his nose violently.

'Mr Finch?'

A soft husky voice came from the darkness above: 'They gone?'

Atticus stepped back and looked up. 'They've gone,' he said. 'Get some sleep, Tom. They won't bother you any more.'

From a different direction, another voice cut crisply through the night: 'You're damn tootin' they won't. Had you covered all the time, Atticus.'

Mr Underwood and a double-barrelled shotgun were leaning out his window above The Maycomb Tribune office.

It was long past my bedtime and I was growing quite tired; it seemed that Atticus and Mr Underwood would talk for the rest of the night, Mr Underwood out the window and Atticus up at him. Finally Atticus returned, switched off the light above the jail door, and picked up his chair.

'Can I carry it for you, Mr Finch?' asked Dill. He had not said a word the whole time.

'Why, thank you, son'.

Walking towards the office, Dill and I fell into step behind Atticus and Jem. Dill was encumbered by the chair, and his pace was slower. Atticus and Jem were well ahead of us, and I assumed that Atticus was giving him hell for not going home but I was wrong. As they passed under a streetlight, Atticus reached out and massaged Jem's hair, his one gesture of affection.

# Roll of Thunder, Hear My Cry

The extract from *Roll of Thunder, Hear My Cry* begins just as the children have helped TJ back to his house. TJ has been used by RW and Melvin Simms to break into the Barnetts' store in Strawberry. When they were disturbed by the Barnetts RW and Melvin brutally attacked them and then turned on TJ when he panicked. They beat him up and forced him to take the pearl-handled pistol he had always wanted. In desperation he has come to Stacey for help.

'Go on, T.J.,' said Stacey. 'We'll wait.'

'Th-thanks, y'all,' T.J. said, then he limped to the side of the house and slipped awkwardly into his room through an open window.

'Come on, let's get out of here,' said Stacey, herding us back to the path. But as we neared the forest, Little Man turned. 'Hey, y'all, look over yonder! What's that?'

Beyond the Avery house bright lights appeared far away on the road near the Granger mansion. For a breathless second they lingered there, then plunged suddenly downward toward the Averys'. The first set of lights was followed by a second, then a third, until there were half a dozen sets of headlights beaming over the trail.

'Wh-what's happening?' cried Christopher-John.

For what seemed an interminable wait, we stood watching those lights drawing nearer and nearer before Stacey clicked off the flashlight and ordered us into the forest. Silently, we slipped into the brush and fell flat to the ground. Two pick-

ups and four cars rattled into the yard, their lights focused like spotlights on the Avery front porch. Noisy, angry men leaped from the cars and surrounded the house.

Kaleb Wallace and his brother Thurston, his left arm hanging akimbo at his side, pounded the front door with their rifle butts. 'Y'all come on outa there!' called Kaleb. 'We want that thieving, murdering nigger of y'all's.'

'St-Stacey,' I stammered, feeling the same nauseous fear I had felt when the night men had passed and when Papa had come home shot and broken, 'wh-what they gonna do?'

'I – I dunno,' Stacey whispered as two more men joined the Wallaces at the door.

'Why, ain't...ain't that R.W. and Melvin?' I exclaimed. 'What the devil they doing –'

Stacey quickly muffled me with the palm of his hand as Melvin thrust himself against the door in an attempt to break it open and R.W. smashed a window with his gun. At the side of the house, several men were climbing through the same window T.J. had entered only a few minutes before. Soon, the front door was flung open from the inside and Mr and Mrs Avery were dragged savagely by their feet from the house. The Avery girls were thrown through the open windows. The older girls, attempting to gather the younger children to them, were slapped back and spat upon. Then quiet, gentle Claude was hauled out, knocked to the ground and kicked.

'C-Claude!' whimpered Christopher-John, trying to rise. But Stacey hushed him and held him down.

'W-we gotta get help,' Stacey rasped, but none of us could move. I watched the world from outside myself.

Then T.J. emerged, dragged from the house on his knees. His face was bloody and when he tried to speak he cried with pain, mumbling his words as if his jaw was broken. Mr Avery tried to rise to get to him, but was knocked back.

'Look what we got here!' one of the men said, holding up a gun. 'That pearl-handled pistol from Jim Lee's store.'

'Oh, Lord,' Stacey groaned. 'Why didn't he get rid of that thing?'

T.J. mumbled something we could not hear and Kaleb Wallace thundered, 'Stop lyin', boy, 'cause you in a whole lot of trouble. You was in there – Miz Barnett, when she come to and got help, said three black boys robbed their store and knocked out her and her husband. And R.W. and Melvin Simms seen you and them two other boys running from behind that store when they come in to town to shoot some pool –'

'But it was R.W. and Melvin –' I started before Stacey clasped his hand over my mouth again.

'–Now who was them other two and where's that money y'all took?'

Whatever T.J.'s reply, it obviously was not what Kaleb Wallace wanted to hear, for he pulled his leg back and kicked T.J.'s swollen stomach with such force that T.J. emitted a cry of awful pain and fell prone upon the ground.

'Lord Jesus! Lord Jesus!' cried Mrs Avery, wrenching herself free from the men who held her and rushing toward her son. 'Don't let 'em hurt my baby no more! Kill me, Lord, but not my child!' But before she could reach T.J., she was caught by the arm and flung so ferociously against the house that she fell, dazed, and Mr Avery, struggling to reach her, was helpless to save either her or T.J.

Christopher-John was sobbing distinctly now. 'Cassie,' Stacey whispered, 'you take Little Man and Christopher-John and y'all–'

The headlights of two more cars appeared in the distance and Stacey immediately hushed. One of the cars halted on the Granger Road, its lights beaming aimlessly into the blackness of the cotton fields, but the lead car came crazy and fast along the rutted trail toward the Avery house, and before it had rolled to a complete stop Mr Jamison leaped out. But once out of the car, he stood very still surveying the scene; then he stared at each of the men as if preparing to charge them in the courtroom and said softly, 'Y'all decide to hold court out here tonight?'

There was an embarrassed silence. Then Kaleb Wallace spoke up. 'Now look here, Mr Jamison, don't you come messin' in this thing.'

'You do,' warned Thurston hotly, 'we just likely to take care of ourselves a nigger lover too tonight.'

An electric tenseness filled the air, but Mr Jamison's placid face was unchanged by the threat. 'Jim Lee Barnett and his wife are still alive. Y'all let the sheriff and me take the boy. Let the law decide whether or not he's guilty.'

'Where's Hank?' someone asked. 'I don't see no law.'

'That's him up at Harlan Granger's,' Mr Jamison said with a wave of his hand over his shoulder. 'He'll be down in a minute. Now leave the boy be.'

'For my money, I say let's do it now,' a voice cried. 'Ain't no need to waste good time and money tryin' no thievin' nigger!'

A crescendo of ugly hate rose from the men as the second car approached. They grew momentarily quiet as the sheriff stepped out. The sheriff looked uneasily at the crowd as if he would rather not be here at all, then at Mr Jamison.

'Where's Harlan?' asked Mr Jamison.

The sheriff turned from Mr Jamison to the crowd without answering him. Then he spoke to the men: 'Mr Granger sent word by me that he ain't gonna stand for no hanging on his place. He say y'all touch one hair on that boy's head while he on this land, he's gonna hold every man here responsible.'

The men took the news in grim silence.

Then Kaleb Wallace cried: 'Then why don't we go somewhere else? I say what we oughta do is take him on down the road and take care of that big black giant of a nigger at the same time!'

'And why not that boy he working for too?' yelled Thurston.

'Stacey!' I gasped.

'Hush!'

A welling affirmation rose from the men. 'I got me three new ropes!' exclaimed Kaleb.

'New? How come you wanna waste a new rope on a nigger? asked Melvin Simms.

'Big as that one nigger is, an old one might break!'

There was chilling laughter and the men moved toward their cars, dragging T.J. with them.

'No!' cried Mr Jamison, rushing to shield T.J. with his own body.

'Cassie,' Stacey whispered hoarsely, 'Cassie, you gotta get Papa now. Tell him what happened. I don't think Mr Jamison can hold them–'

'You come too.'

'No, I'll wait here.'

'I ain't going without you!' I declared, afraid that he would do something stupid like trying to rescue T.J. alone.

'Look, Cassie, go on, will ya please? Papa'll know what to do. Somebody's gotta stay here case they take T.J. off into the woods somewhere. I'll be all right.'

'Well...'

'Please, Cassie? Trust me, will ya?'

I hesitated. 'Y-you promise you won't go down there by yourself?'

'Yeah, I promise. Just get Papa and Mr Morrison 'fore they – 'fore they hurt them some more.' He placed the unlit flashlight in my hand and pushed me up. Clutching Little Man's hand, I told him to grab Christopher-John's, and together the three of us picked our way along the black path, afraid to turn on the flashlight for fear of its light being seen.

Thunder crashed against the corners of the world and lightning split the sky as we reached the road, but we did not stop. We dared not. We had to reach Papa.

## COMPARING THE TWO EXTRACTS

The novels from which these extracts are taken are set at about the same time (the mid-1930's) and in the same area (the Deep South). They both deal with relations between white and black people and with the injustice with which black people were faced. Both of them were written by women and are based on their knowledge of real events in the past. Both use young girls to tell their stories.

It is interesting to compare these two books and to think about the important *differences* between them as well as the similarities.

This activity concentrates just on the extracts from the novels. Have a look at the questions below. Talk about them and try to decide how your answers would be similar/different for the two extracts. You might want to write short notes rather than full answers to each question.

1 **Where does each passage take place?**

2 **Why are the children there?**

3 **What do we learn about the 'nightriders'? Choose 3/4 words or phrases from the passage that sum up their mood.**

4 **Who does most of the talking?**

5 **Who is in control of the situation?**

6 **At what point(s) is there serious danger for the character(s) involved?**

7 **What is the climax of each passage?**

8 **How much do we learn about the person the nightriders are wanting to get at?**

9 **Is the danger overcome?**

10 **What three or four words or phrases would you use to sum up the mood of each passage?**

Using the notes you have made try writing a comparison of the two extracts. Say which of the two you find more powerful – and why.

(Of course, if you've read the whole of *To Kill a Mockingbird,* you could write a lot more...)

*Roll of Thunder, Hear My Cry* ends with these three paragraphs.

# THE ENDING

**In the afternoon when I awakened, or tomorrow or the next day, the boys and I would still be free to run the red road, to wander through the old forest and sprawl lazily on the banks of the pond. Come October, we would trudge to school as always, barefooted and grumbling, fighting the dust and the mud and the Jefferson Davis school bus. But T.J. never would again.**

**I had never liked T.J., but he had always been there, a part of me, a part of my life, just like the mud and the rain, and I had thought that he always would be. Yet the mud and the rain and the dust would all pass. I knew and understood that. What had happened to T.J. in the night I did not understand, but I knew that it would not pass. And I cried for those things which had happened in the night and would not pass.**

**I cried for T.J. For T.J. and the land.**

How have things changed for Cassie and the Logan family since the beginning of the book? How do you as a reader feel about what has happened by the end of the story?

The statements below give the reactions of different readers to the ending of the book. Discuss each one and decide which statement best matches your feeling about the ending. If you can't find one that is close enough, write a statement of your own.

**1** *I found the end of the book confusing and depressing. It ends on Cassie – and she is confused and depressed by what has happened. Because she is young she can't understand it and can't cope with it. That's the feeling I got from it too.*

**2** *It's hard to know what to think at the end. The book doesn't really end: it just stops and leaves everything hanging in mid-air, with both TJ and the Logan's land at risk. In both cases we don't know what's going to happen.*

**3** *What we learn at the end of the story is just that the Logans have survived. That makes it a kind of a happy ending. It may not seem much of a high point to end on – but in the dangerous world they live in they do well just to survive.*

**4** *It's very sad at the end, I thought. Sad not because of TJ who doesn't count for much, but sad because Cassie, who starts out hopeful and carefree, ends up feeling so heavy. She has learned that there is nothing in their life to feel hopeful about.*

**5** *Although in the course of the story things go from bad to worse, oddly enough I didn't find the ending depressing. I think that's because of what you see on the way: you see Cassie learning about her parents; you see their determination to hang on to their land and make a better life eventually; you see people living under oppression but fighting against it.*

NOTE
*Roll of Thunder, Hear My Cry* is not the end of the story of Cassie and the Logan family. The story continues in a sequel called *Let the Circle Be Unbroken* – also published by Puffin.

# THE COVER

The pictures used on the hardback and paperback editions of *Roll of Thunder, Hear My Cry* are paintings rather than photographs. Suppose you were doing a new cover for the book and you had the photographs below to choose from. All the photographs were taken in the American South during the 1930's – most of them by photographers working for government agencies which were gathering information about living conditions.

Which photograph would you use to give an impression of what the book is about? What order of preference would you put the rest of the photographs in?

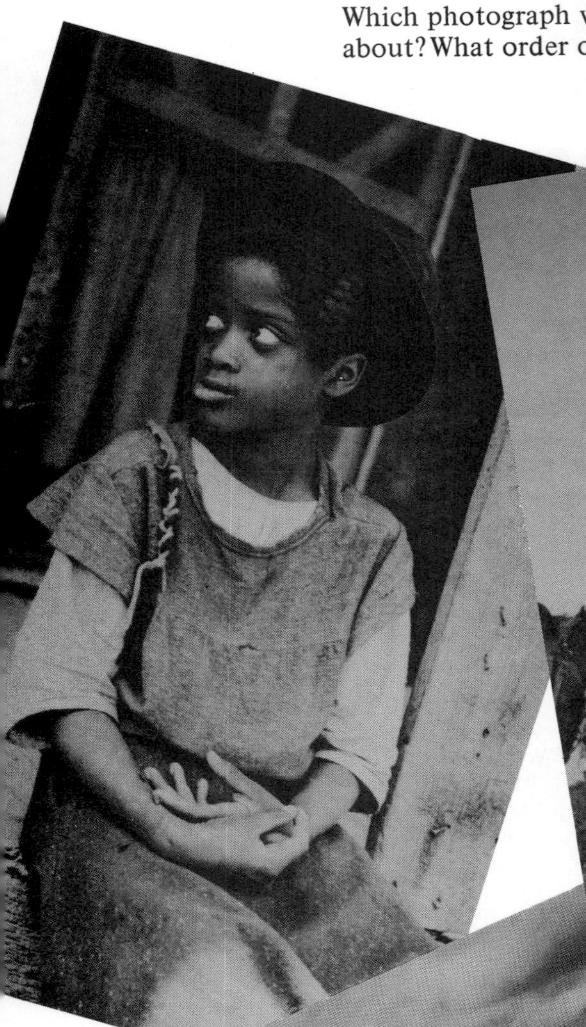

# I THINK...

**Here are some extracts from comments made by reviewers of *Roll of Thunder, Hear My Cry* when it was first published. They concentrate on different aspects of the novel — and some contradict one another.**

**Read through the extracts and decide how far you agree with the points made in each of them: do you agree *completely, to some extent* or *not at all*?**

**1** *The commitment of the Logan family to one another and to their land is the central theme of this book. Their strength, warmth and unity against all odds is evident from the first page to the last. It is a story about the family not the individuals in it.*

**2** *The novel is a powerful and dramatic documentary of a period in black history. It brings to life the experience of a generation of black people in the Southern states: the experience, seen from a black point of view, which 'history books' usually ignore. I have no doubt that many black readers in America, young and old will enjoy and admire the book. White readers may not have so much to identify with.*

**3** *One of the major problems about this book is that Cassie is the storyteller. She can't be in two places at once and this leads to difficulties in the structure of the story. All too often the reader has to depend on second-hand descriptions when a direct account of the event itself would be preferable. This even happens in the climax of the book when we are kept from seeing the fire.*

**4** *What struck me most was to be reminded how important education was to these people and what a struggle they had to win the right to education. Nowadays we take education too much for granted — and isn't it sadly the case that some young people now don't believe in it at all?*

**5** *This book had me in two minds: hoping that Stacey and Cassie would get their own back but worrying about the consequences if they did; admiring the determination of their father and mother, but fearing that their efforts would be unsuccessful.*

**6** *As far as use in schools is concerned, I don't think I would recommend it. The book dwells on the divisions between black and white — and its message is harsh. We are at a different stage now in the relationship between black and white — and I believe the pupils in our schools need a different message. In other words, a book like this may do more harm than good.*

**FOR WRITING**

What do you think about the book as a whole? What comments would you want to make about it?

Make a list of the points you would want to mention. Then choose some episodes from the book to use as evidence for what you want to say.

Using your list of points and your selection of episodes, write about your view of the book.

# BLACK AMERICAN HISTORY: further reading

**In this list we have provided a small amount of information about some of the women and men who fought against slavery in America and some of the women and men who, later, fought for civil rights for black people. In most cases there are some suggestions for books you could look at if you want to find out more about these people. (Some of these books are quite difficult reading.) The list of names could be very much longer.**

## Against slavery

**Olaudah Equiano 1745-1801**
He was taken as a slave from Africa to America at the age of 11. After travelling the world as servant to a ship's captain, he bought his freedom in 1776. Later he wrote his life-story which was powerful evidence in the anti-slavery movement.

*Equiano's Travels* ed. P. Edwards 0435900102
*Olaudah Equiano* H. Sinclair, LMS 'Explore-a-story'.
*Discovering Africa's Past* B. Davidson 0582220491
*Black Settlers in Britain 1555-1958* N. File & C. Power 0435311735

*Slaves spreading the news of their liberation in 1863.*

**David Walker 1785-?**
He was born free and became a shopkeeper and journalist. Because of an anti-slavery pamphlet that he wrote, his life was threatened by angry whites. He refused to back down and soon after disappeared without trace.
*The Negro People in American History*, W.Z. Foster, 0717802760
*Great Negroes Past and Present*, R.L. Adams, 0910030081

**Sojourner Truth 1797-1883**
She grew up as a slave in New York State and was freed in 1827. She became a preacher and a campaigner for the abolition of slavery and for women's rights. She was famous as an extraordinarily good speaker.
*Sojourner Truth: Fearless Crusader*, H.S. Peterson 0811645746
*Women Race and Class* A. Davis 0704338920
*Black Women in White America*, ed. G. Lerner 0394718801

**Nat Turner 1800-1831**
He was a slave who illegally learnt to read. In 1831 he led a slave revolt in which a number of whites were killed. The rebellion was crushed, however, and Nat Turner was hanged.
*World's Great Men of Colour* (Volume 2), J.A. Rogers 0020813104
*The People Who Came* (Book 3), E. Braithwaite & A. Phillips 0582763142
*Great Negroes Past and Present*, R.L. Adams 0910030081

**Harriet Tubman 1820-1913**
She was born a slave but escaped to the North and finally to Canada. She worked for the 'Underground Railroad' – a network of secret escape routes for runaway slaves. Altogether she helped more than 300 slaves to escape. During the Civil War she acted as a nurse, spy and guerrilla leader for the Northern side.
*Harriet Tubman: Guide to Freedom* S. & L. Epstein, Garrad Publishing Company
*Women Race and Class* A. Davis 0704338920
*Black Women in White America* , ed. G. Lerner 0394718801
*The Slave Trade,* J. Kamm 0237292297
*Let My People Go,* J.G. Gittings 071750056X

**Frederick Douglass 1818-1895**
He was born a slave, son of an African mother and a white father. When he grew up, he escaped to New York where he became a leading campaigner for the

Abraham Lincoln

abolition of slavery. He was also a strong supporter of women's rights.

*Narrative of the Life of Frederick Douglass, an American Slave,* ed. H.A. Baker 014039012X
*World's Great Men of Colour* (Volume 2), J.A. Rogers 0020813104
*The People Who Came* (Book 3), E. Braithwaite and A. Phillips 0582763142
*Women Race and Class,* A. Davis 0704338920

**Levi Coffin 1979-1877**
He was a white Quaker leader and abolitionist. He and his wife sheltered hundreds of escaped slaves in their house and helped them to freedom. He became known as 'the President' of the Underground Railroad.
*Underground to Canada,* B. Smucker 014031122X

**John Brown 1800-1859**
He was a white man who fought for the abolition of slavery. In 1859 he seized a federal armoury near Harpers Ferry, intending to set up a stronghold for escaped slaves. He was forced to surrender by U.S. Marines and hanged.
*John Brown,* W.E.B. DuBois 0717803759
*The Slaves,* S. Everett 0861240111

**Prudence Crandall 1803-1890**
She was a white schoolteacher in Canterbury, Connecticut, who accepted a black girl into her school. When white parents took their children away, she enrolled more black girls. Vicious attacks were made on the school and finally she was arrested.

**Abraham Lincoln 1809-1865**
He was President of the US during the American Civil War. In 1863 he declared that the slaves in the eleven rebel Southern states must be set free, but this did not actually happen until the end of the Civil War in 1865. Lincoln was assassinated in 1865.

**Alexander Milton Ross 1832-1897**
He was a white abolitionist who decided at an early age to help slaves escape to Canada. Posing as a bird-watcher, he talked to slaves working on plantations and gave them money and information.
*Underground to Canada,* B. Smucker 0140309039

**Ida B. Wells 1862-1931**
She was a famous journalist who for many years carried out a crusade against lynching and spent her life campaigning against injustice and racism. She was a founder member of the National Association for the Advancement of Coloured Peoples.
*Women, Race and Class,* A. Davis 0704338920
*Black Women in White America,* ed. G. Lerner 0394718801
*Great Negroes Past and Present,* R.L. Adams 0910030081

**Mary Church Terrell 1863-1954**
She spent her life campaigning for equal rights for blacks and for women. At the age of 89 she took an active part in the desegregation of restaurants in her home town of Washington.
*Women Race and Class,* A. Davis 0704338920
*Black Women in White America,* ed. G. Lerner 0394718801
*Great Negroes Past and Present,* R.L. Adams 0910030081

Frederick Douglass

W.E.B. Du Bois

**W.E.B. DuBois 1868-1963**
He was a famous campaigner and writer against racism. He insisted that black people should be proud of themselves and their heritage. He was a founder member of the National Association for the Advancement of Coloured Peoples.
*World's Great Men of Colour,* J.A. Rogers, Collier Books 0020813104
*A History of West Africa AD1000 To The Present,* M. Crowder and G. Abdullahi 0582603684
*The People Who Came* (Book 3), E. Braithwaite & A.Phillips 0582763142
*Great Negroes Past and Present,* R.L. Adams 0910030081

# For Civil Rights

Marcus Garvey

**Marcus Garvey 1887-1940**
He was born in Jamaica. As a young man he was an active trade unionist but later came to believe that black people's best hope lay in emigration to Africa. After the failure of his 'Black Star Line' shipping company he returned to politics and trade unionism but made little progress against the white rulers of Jamaica at that time. He finally died in England.
*Marcus Garvey 1887-1940,* A. Edwards, New Beacon Books
National Heroes, Honours and Awards. Published by the Agency for Public Information, 58A Halfway Tree Road, Kingston 10.
*A History of West Africa AD 1000 to The Present,* M. Crowder and G. Abdullahi 0582603684
*World's Great Men of Colour* (Vol 2), J.A. Rogers 0020813104
*The People Who Came* (Book 3), E. Braithwaite & A. Phillips 0582763142
*Marcus Garvey,* LMS 'Explore-a-story'

**Paul Robeson 1898-1976**
He was a brilliant student who qualified as a lawyer, became an American football player and later an actor and singer. In 1947 he sacrificed his career to fight for black people's rights. The American government confiscated his passport and prevented him from working in theatres, concert halls and elsewhere.
*World's Great Men of Colour* (Vol 2), J.A. Rogers 0020813104
*Being Black,* ed. R. Harris 0901241393

**Malcolm X 1925-1965**
Born Malcolm Little, his early life of drugs and crime in New York led him to prison. On his release he joined the Nation of Islam and in time became one of its leaders and a militant figure for black rights and black separatism. After a pilgrimage to Mecca he left the Nation of Islam and formed 'The Organisation of Afro-American Unity'. In 1965 he was murdered.
*Malcolm X: Black and Proud,* F.M. White 0811645827
*Malcolm X,* A. Adoff 0690514158
*Being Black,* Roxy Harris 0901241393
*The People Who Came* (Book 3), E. Braithwaite & A. Phillips 0582763142

**Coretta Scott King 1927-**
She married Martin Luther King in 1953 and worked with him on all his campaigns. She wrote a book with him about the Montgomery Bus Boycott, *Stride towards Freedom.* After his assassination, she carried on his work. She is President of the Martin Luther King, Jr., Centre for Social Change.
*Coretta Scott King,* L. Patterson 0811645851
*The Battle of Boston,* J. Hillson 0873484711

**Martin Luther King 1929-1968**
He was a church minister who became a Civil Rights leader. In 1955 he led the Montgomery Bus Boycott against segregated buses, and went on to lead black (and white) people in non-violent action for black civil rights. In 1963, at the massive Civil Rights March on Washington, he made his famous speech: 'I have a dream today'. In 1968 he was assassinated.
*Martin Luther King: The Peaceful Warrior,* ed. E. Clayton 067142869
*The Words of Martin Luther King Jr.,* ed. C.S. King 0860512789
*The People Who Came* (Book 3), E. Braithwaite & A. Phillips 0582763142
*Great Negroes Past and Present,* R.L. Adams 910030081

**Angela Davis 1944-**
She became a target for the American government in the 1960's because of her involvement with the Black Power movement. She was arrested in 1972 and tried on trumped up charges of providing guns for a raid on a court house, but was acquitted. She is now a lecturer, writer and political activist.
*If They Come in the Morning,* A. Davis 0855140062
*Angela Davis: An Autobiography,* 0099133601
*Black Women in White America,* ed. G. Lerner 0394718801
*Soledad Brothers,* G. Jackson 0140033157
*Patterns of Racism* (Book Two), 0850010241

# Suggestions for further research

**This list gives the titles of books which may be useful if you would like to do some more research on aspects of black history.**

## AFRICA

The slave trade made European countries very rich and the countries of Africa and the West Indies very poor. When white people first went to Africa in the 15th century, they were amazed to see great cities, splendid palaces, and the very rich way that many Africans lived. They heard about the great empires of Ghana, Mali, Kongo and Zimbabwe. They heard about important discoveries made at the West African Universities of Jenne and Timbuktu. They saw the beautiful bronze works of art from Benin and Ife in Nigeria. So at first they traded with Africa as equals. If you would like to know more about Africa's history you could refer to the following books:

*Guide to African History,* B. Davidson 004960001X
*A History of West Africa AD 1000 to the Present,* M. Crowder and G. Abdullahi 0582603684
*Discovering Africa's Past,* B. Davidson 0582220491
*A Visual History of Africa,* E. Loftus 0237500256
*A Plague of Europeans,* D. Killingray 0140806717
*Treasures of Ancient Nigeria,* E. Eyo and F. Willett 0002170868
*World's Great Men of Colour* (Volume 1), 0020813007
*Women Leaders in African History,* D. Sweetman 0435944800

## SLAVERY

Africans were brought to America as slaves and were used in all states. But it was in the Southern states that they were used in huge numbers in order to work on the rice, tobacco and cotton plantations. In spite of the harsh laws which controlled slaves and the cruel and severe punishments inflicted upon them, they did not accept their position meekly. The slaves fought back, they resisted, escaped, rebelled and campaigned for their freedom. If you want to find out more about what they did you could look at some of the following books:

*Many Thousand Gone: The Ex-Slaves' Account of their Bondage and Freedom,* C.H. Nichols 0253201330
*The Slaves,* S. Everett 0086124011
*American Negro Slave Revolts,* H. Aptheker 0717800032
*The People Who Came* (Book 3), E. Braithwaite & A. Phillips 0582763142
*West Africa and the Atlantic Slave Trade,* W. Rodney, The Walter Rodney Bookshop
*Narrative of the Life of Frederick Douglass,* ed. H.A. Baker Jr. 014039012X
*Equiano's Travels,* ed. P. Edwards 04359000102
*The Slave Trade,* D. Killingray
*Make Free: The Story of the Underground Railroad,* W. Breyfogle, Lippincott
*Black Women in White America,* ed. G. Lerner 0394718801
*Roots,* A. Haley 033025018
*The Colour Purple,* A. Walker 0704339056
*Underground to Canada,* B. Smucker 014031122X
*Long Journey Home,* J. Lester 0140309039
*To Be A Slave,* J. Lester
*A Taste of Freedom,* J. Lester 0582201284

## CIVIL RIGHTS

The abolition of slavery did not bring about equality or social justice for black people but a different kind of exploitation. They were given the worst jobs, the worst housing and the worst schools – but many black people formed themselves into organizations to fight for equal rights. The civil rights movement after the Second World War period was enormously important and influential. You could find out more about some of the following people and events by looking at the books below.

- Rosa Parks and the Montgomery bus boycott
- Birmingham Sunday, September 15th 1963.
- Elizabeth Eckford and Little Rock Central High School
- Martin Luther King and CORE (the Congress of Racial Equality)
- 1963 and the March on Washington
- Malcolm X and the Black Muslims
- The trial of Angela Davis
- The Soledad Brothers
- The Detroit Riot of 1967
- Black athletes at the 1968 Mexico Olympics
- Huey Newton, Bobby Seale and the Black Panther Party

*Being Black,* R. Harris 0901241393
*Soledad Brothers: The Prison Letters of George Jackson,* 0140033157
*Angela Davis: An Autobiography,* 0099133601
*Patterns of Racism* (Book 2), 0850010241
*Stride Toward Freedom: The Montgomery Story,* Martin Luther King Jr.
*Martin Luther King: The Peaceful Warrior,* ed. Ed Clayton 067141869
*Malcolm X,* A. Adoff 0690514158
*Malcolm X Black and Proud,* F.M. White 0811645827
*The Battle of Boston,* J. Hillson 0873484711
*The People Who Came* (Book 3), E. Braithwaite and A. Phillips 0582763142
*If They Come In The Morning,* A. Davis 0855140062
*Coretta Scott King,* L. Patterson 0811645851
*Black Lives White Worlds,* ed. K. Ajegbo 0521284635

# Acknowledgements

This booklet incorporates material which appeared in an earlier booklet on *Roll of Thunder, Hear My Cry* produced at Thomas Tallis School by Kate Blackwell, Simon Lee, Geoff Parker and Jackie Payne in collaboration with Danny Padmore of the ILEA Multi-Ethnic advisory team. The booklet has also made use of material devised on an English Centre course by Clare Gilman, Maureen Davies, Anita Miles, Christine Burton, Sheila Goodesham and Sandra Peate. Further contributions were made by Wendy Weinstock, Hugh Betterton and Danny Padmore.

The final stage of editing and writing was undertaken by Jane Leggett, Elizabeth Plackett, Mike Raleigh and Helen Savva.

We are grateful to those publishers and organizations who have given permission to use extracts and photographs in the lists below. We would be pleased to hear from any holders of copyright whom we have been unable to contact. Thanks to Chris Brookeman, Polytechnic of Central London American Studies Resources Centre, for help with illustrative material.

**We are grateful for permission to quote extracts from the following texts:**
From *Black Boy* by Richard Wright, published in the U.K. by Longman Group Ltd., to John Farquharson Ltd. From the Newbery Award Acceptance Speech 1977 by Mildred D. Taylor, to the author. From the recollections of Elizabeth Eckford included in the notes to *Black Protest,* by permission of Educational Audio Visual Inc., Pleasantville, NY 10570. From *Coming of Age in Mississippi* by Anne Moody, a Dial Press Book, by permission of Doubleday & Company, Inc. From 'A College on A Garbage Dump' by Mary McLeod Bethune, included in *Black Women in White America: A Documentary History* ed. by Gerda Lerner, to Pantheon Books, a division of Random House, Inc. From *Echo in My Soul* by Septima Clark, to E.P. Dutton, Inc. From *To Kill a Mockingbird* by Harper Lee, by permission of William Heinemann Ltd. From *Roll of Thunder, Hear My Cry* by Mildred D. Taylor, to the U.K. publisher Victor Gollancz Ltd.

**The photographs on the following pages are from the collection made for the U.S. Farm Security Adminstration 1935–1938 and held in the public domain by the Library of Congress. The photographer's name is given where this is known.**
Inside front cover, Evans; page 1 Evans; page 5 Lange; page 6 Evans (top Lange); page 7 (including bottom right and left Evans); page 8 Evans; page 9 (including top left and right Evans); page 10 (including top left Lange, top right and centre Evans); page 17 Evans; page 19; page 28 (top) Evans; page 29 (top right Lee, left Evans); page 30 Evans; page 31 Evans; page 32 Lee; page 33; page 35 Evans; page 42 (including top left Lee); inside back cover. The sequences of FSA photographs by Walker Evans on pages 8 – 9 and page 30 are reproduced from *Walker Evans At Work,* Thames and Hudson Ltd.

**The sources of other photographs and illustrations are as follows:**
Page 4 (bottom left) and page 14 (top right and bottom left), *Ebony* Magazine – all reproduced in *Patterns of Racism* (Book 2), Institute of Race Relations. Cover, Chicago Historical Society; Page 45(top), Library of Congress – reproduced in *Abraham Lincoln* by Lord Longford,gford, Weidenfeld and Nicholson. Page 13 (right), page 14 (top left) and page 25, UPI; page 11 (top right), U.S. Army; page 45 (bottom) and page 46, Culver Collection – all reproduced in *Struggle for Freedom* by D.S. Davis, Harcourt Brace Jovanovich Inc. Page 9 (bottom right); page 11 (left), Library of Congress – reproduced in *An Album of the Great Depression* by W.L. Katz, Franklin Watts. Page 12, Black Star; page 13 (left), Associated Press Photos – reproduced in *Martin Luther King* by Patricia Baker, Wayland. Page 27, from *The Plantation South,* Polytechnic of Central London American Studies Resources Centre. Pages 37 and 38, from the film *To Kill a Mockingbird,* MCA Publishing Division, copyright by Universal Pictures (a division of Universal City Studios). Cover, jacket illustration by David Leeming – Victor Gollancz Ltd.

**Designed by Margaret Dodd**
**Published by The English *& Media* Centre, 136 Chalton Street, London NW1 1RX.**
**Orders to NATE, 50 Broadfield Road, Broadfield Business Centre, Sheffield S8 0XJ.**

**Printed in Great Britain by BPC Wheatons Ltd. Exeter.**